# Fantasy Football for Smart People

## Daily Fantasy Pros Reveal Their Money-Making Secrets

Jonathan Bales

All Rights Reserved ©2014

Jonathan Bales. First Printing: 2014. The editorial arrangement, analysis, and professional commentary are subject to this copyright notice. No portion of this book may be copied, retransmitted, reposted, duplicated, or otherwise used without the express written approval of the author, except by reviewers who may quote brief excerpts in connection with a review.

United States laws and regulations are public domain and not subject to copyright. Any unauthorized copying, reproduction, translation, or distribution of any part of this material without permission by the author is prohibited and against the law.

Disclaimer and Terms of Use: Your reliance upon information and content obtained by you at or through this publication is solely at your own risk. The author assumes no liability or responsibility for damage or injury to you, other persons, or property arising from any use of any product, information, idea, or instruction contained in the content or services provided to you through this book. Reliance upon information contained in this material is solely at the reader's own risk. The authors have no financial interest in and receive no compensation from manufacturers of products or websites mentioned in this book.

# Table of Contents

*Fantasy Football for Smart People: Daily Fantasy Pros Reveal Their Money-Making Secrets*

## Chapter 5: Winning Cash Games with PrimeTime420

- How to pick players specifically to win cash games
- How to handle defense/kicker
- Stats on which positions work best in the flex

## Chapter 6: Advanced Tournament Play with Al_Smizzle

- How to improve your chances of winning a GPP
- Understanding when to be contrarian
- How and when to stack

## Chapter 7: Lineup Creation with Naapstermaan

- How to alter your lineup based on your league
- Scoring in Thursday-night games
- Pairing players in the optimal way

## Chapter 8: Building a Bankroll with KillaB2482

- How to easily manage your bankroll
- Why there's no one-size-fits-all plan
- Understanding player exposure and risk

## **Bonus Material: How to Win Heads-Up Leagues and 50/50s

- The typical scores needed to win on DraftKings
- How to properly allocate cap space
- Understanding player types and why they matter

## Preface

Abraham Lincoln once said, "It doesn't matter if a cat is black or white; as long as it can catch mice, it's a good cat." Actually, he didn't say that. It was a random quote that I found on the internet. But it sounds so much better when I envision A.L. saying it.

When I wrote my last book on daily fantasy sports—*Fantasy Football for Smart People: How to Turn Your Hobby into a Fortune*—the goal was to throw as much awesome data at you as possible. Like many books in my *Fantasy Football for Smart People* series, that one was highly analytical and meant to take subjectivity out of equation as much as possible. I worked with DraftKings, and they provided me with all of the information on what's actually winning leagues on the site. In effect, I wanted to know if the cat was black or white. And if her name was Billie Jean.

This book is going to take an approach different from my past work. I've interviewed some of the top players in daily fantasy sports on all of the foundational daily fantasy concepts—league selection, projections, bankroll management, and so on. The goal—to slowly uncover the most effective way to go about winning money playing daily fantasy football—is still the same as always.

This time, though, I'm trying to figure out how the cats catch their mice. If there's "absolute" Truth with a capital 'T' and truth in practicality, this book will try to combine the two forms—an attempt to blend the objective and subjective in daily fantasy football.

The daily fantasy pros who have helped me along the way were each assigned to a specific chapter, which comes in the form of an interview, plus additional analysis. That analysis is broken up into two parts—the latter from me and the former from daily fantasy pro "CSURAM88," aka Peter Jennings.

Peter has helped me on previous books, and he's one of the top all-around daily fantasy players in the world. RotoGrinders—a daily fantasy content site that has a bunch of awesome tools and imports site data to rank players—has Peter as a top 10 player in NFL, MLB, and NBA, as well as the fifth-ranked player in the world.

| Rankings | CSURAM88 |
|---|---|
| Overall updates weekly on Thursday. | |
| Overall Ranking | 5th (274621.46) |
| TPOY Ranking | 6th (15235.22) |
| Monthly Grinder Leaderboard | 5th (12275.98) |
| NFL Grinder Leaderboard | 8th (33634.39) |
| MLB Grinder Leaderboard | 6th (49175.45) |
| NBA Grinder Leaderboard | 6th (94417.15) |

Peter won the 2012 FFFC—and a $150,000 grand prize—to become the first six-figure prize-winner in daily fantasy history. Fast-forward just a couple years and the prize pools have become ridiculous; we'll see DraftKings make numerous users instant millionaires this year.

To complement the interviews and Peter's analysis, I'll offer some of the data I've collected recently that fits with the topic of each chapter. As much as I think there's value in learning from experience (especially in daily fantasy sports), I'm still data-driven at heart, so hopefully those numbers can shed some light on the discussions.

In addition to my *Fantasy Football for Smart People* books, I also sell a variety of other fantasy-related packages. If you're playing daily fantasy football this season (or just season-long), the most useful to you might be my Weekly In-Season Package. With that, you'll receive:

- UNLIMITED advice all year
- Customizable projections for every relevant player, all 17 weeks of the season
- Optimized daily fantasy football values with player salaries
- Weekly newsletter with analysis

Those who purchased the package last year saw big results. Actually, one user cashed $25,000 in two tournaments! I also sell a season-long fantasy football draft package, along with all of my books, at FantasyFootballDrafting.com.

And finally, consider enrolling in RotoAcademy—my fantasy football training school. For just a few bucks per month, RotoAcademy will deliver you year-round, book-length (yes, book-length) fantasy football analysis. I write the majority of the content—provided via monthly newsletters sent right to your email—but there are a few other really talented instructors as well. I personally promise that it will make you a significantly better fantasy owner, or I'll give you your money back.

Not sure if you want to enroll? Test it first. You can download free RotoAcademy lessons right here. Thanks for your support, and best of luck this season!

## Some Free Fantasy Football Stuff for You

I like giving things away, so here's some stuff for you. The first is 10 percent off anything you purchase on my site—all books, all rankings, my draft package, the Weekly In-Season Package with DFS Values, and even past issues of RotoAcademy. Just go to FantasyFootballDrafting.com and use the code **"Smart10"** at checkout to get the savings.

The second freebie is an entire issue of RotoAcademy. Why an entire issue for free? Because I'm really excited about this product and I think if you start reading, you'll be hooked and become a full-time student. Remember, this is a year-long training course that's absolutely guaranteed to turn you into a dominant fantasy owner.

Go to FantasyFootballDrafting.com for your free issue (RotoAcademy Issue II), add the item to your cart, and enter "RA100" at checkout to get it free of charge.

Finally, I've partnered with DraftKings to give you a 100 percent deposit bonus when you sign up there. Deposit $500 and then bam! you got $1,000. DraftKings is the main site where I play daily fantasy football. Deposit there at DraftKings.com/Bales to get the bonus, use the "Smart10" code to buy my in-season package at FantasyFootballDrafting.com (complete with DraftKings values all year long), and start cashing in on your hobby.

Like I said, a whole lot of readers profited last year with my in-season package; who couldn't use an extra $50k? There's an outstanding investment opportunity in daily fantasy sports right now, and there's really no reason for you *not* to get involved.

Before getting to the first interview, feel free to look over the following daily fantasy glossary.

# A Daily Fantasy Glossary

There are a whole bunch of terms specific to the daily fantasy realm that aren't used among season-long fantasy owners. I use a lot of these terms throughout the book, so I've created a glossary to which you can refer if you're unsure what the hell I'm talking about.

### +EV

Positive Expected Value; a situation in which you expect a positive return on your investment. Daily fantasy players are constantly searching for +EV situations.

### $/Point

Dollars per point; the number of dollars you must spend (in cap space) for every point a player is projected to score. A lower $/point is preferable.

### 50/50

A league type in which the top half of all entrants get paid and the bottom half lose their entry fee. 50/50 leagues are generally considered safe, but they can become dangerous if you enter the same lineup into multiple leagues.

### Bankroll

The amount of money you're willing to invest in daily fantasy sports

### Bearish

A pessimistic outlook on a particular player, team, or situation. If you're bearish on a player, you wouldn't use him in your lineups.

### Bullish

The opposite of bearish; an optimistic outlook on a particular situation. If you're bullish on a player, you'd use him in your daily fantasy lineups.

### Buy-In

The amount of money needed to enter a particular league

### Cash Game

A head-to-head, 50/50, multi-match, or three-man daily fantasy league

### Ceiling

A player, team, or lineup's upside; the maximum number of points they could score

### Chalk

The favorite; the popular pick

### Commission

The fee charged by the daily fantasy sites to play in a league; typically around 10 percent of the total buy-ins

### Contrarian

An against-the-grain strategy used by daily fantasy players in tournaments; seeks to identify low-usage players who are flying under-the-radar, "overpriced," or otherwise won't be in many lineups

### DFS

Acronym for daily fantasy sports

### Exposure

The amount of money invested in a player; if you have a lot of exposure to a particular player, it means you have a relatively high percentage of your bankroll placed on him.

### Fade

To avoid a particular player or game, i.e. "I'm fading the Patriots game because there are 30 MPH winds."

### Floor

A player, team, or lineup's downside; the minimum number of points they could score

### Freeroll

A daily fantasy league that's free to enter but has cash prizes

### GPP

"Guaranteed Prize Pool"; a league in which the prize is guaranteed, regardless of the number of entrants

### Head-to-head (Heads-Up)

A one-one-one daily fantasy league

### Hedge

Actions taken to reduce the overall risk of your lineups; if you're excessively bullish on a particular lineup, for example, you would hedge by creating other lineups without any of the same players, even if it's sub-optimal. When you hedge, you're reducing risk at the cost of also reducing upside.

### High-Low
Also known as "stars and scrubs"; when you select multiple elite, high-salary players to accompany low-priced, bargain bin players (in contrast to a balanced strategy)

### Model
Any mathematical system used to project players and/or optimize lineups

### Multiplier
A league in which you can multiply your entry fee by a certain factor based on the payouts; in a 5x multiplier, for example, the winners get paid out five times their entry fee. The higher the multiplier, the more high-risk/high-reward the league.

### Overlay
When a daily fantasy site loses money on a GPP; if $20,000 is guaranteed but there are only $18,000 worth of entrants, the overlay is $2,000.

### PPR
Point per reception; a scoring system that provides a point for all catches and dramatically influences strategy

### Qualifier
A league in which the winners don't receive cash, but rather win a "ticket" into another league; a 10-team qualifier with an $11 buy-in might give away one ticket into a larger league with a $100 buy-in, for example; in opposition to cash games

### Reach

To select a player who doesn't provide great value, i.e. a high $/point; reaches typically result in -EV (negative expected value) situations

### ROI

Return on Investment

### Stacking

To pair multiple players from the same professional team in an effort to increase upside; stacking is particularly popular in daily fantasy baseball

# Chapter 1: Research with Headchopper

At its core, daily fantasy football is about transforming research into quality lineups, and the best players find a way to research in the most efficient ways possible. To discuss the research aspect of daily fantasy sports, I spoke with Headchopper—widely considered one of the game's most elite players. He's the 2013 DFBBC Champion, a three-time FFFC finalist, a two-time DFFC finalist, PFBC finalist, PFFC finalist, and DSBBC finalist. He was also the runner-up for 2012 Tournament Player of the Year.

Headchopper has been ranked near the top of the RotoGrinders leaderboards since 2009, as high as the No. 3 overall daily fantasy player in the world. Here's a look at his current ranks in each sport.

| Rankings | Headchopper |
| --- | --- |
| Overall updates weekly on Thursday. | |
| Overall Ranking | 21$^{st}$ (96335.37) |
| TPOY Ranking | 3$^{rd}$ (19118.41) |
| Monthly Grinder Leaderboard | 43$^{rd}$ (985.42) |
| NFL Grinder Leaderboard | 19$^{th}$ (17377.89) |
| MLB Grinder Leaderboard | 24$^{th}$ (14676.45) |
| NBA Grinder Leaderboard | 35$^{th}$ (22185.70) |

Currently ranked as a top 20 NFL player in the world, Headchopper is more than qualified to dish out daily fantasy research advice.

## What are your favorite sites to use when researching for daily fantasy football?

My favorite is probably RotoGrinders. They have so many awesome tools and everything is right there, man. I like to use the tools to check player values and see what some of the other experts are thinking. And I can check a lot of different stats right there too—targets, red zone stats, stuff like that.

Pro Football Focus also has some good information. That's really a nice blend of stats and film, and I'm just as much of a film guy for football as stats, so that's helpful stuff. It's nice to see the stuff you see on film quantified, and they have a lot of unique stats like air yards and yards before contact. I also check out Football Outsiders, which is a similar type of thing, although more stats-based.

But like I said, I really prefer to watch film whenever possible because sometimes NFL stats can be a little misleading, so I subscribe to NFL Game Rewind. That allows me to go back and watch any game, and you can also check out the coaches' film, which is nice. That's really the biggest thing for me. I really like to watch the footage; sometimes the stats can be really helpful but sometimes you just need to see what's going on.

In terms of reading analysis and stuff like that, I don't really do too much of it. My research is mainly just looking up different stats and watching the games. I have a few other players whose opinions I trust, so I consult with them and I'll read their stuff from time to time if they write, but for the most part I kind of like to do my own thing.

There's so much information out there that everything gets so watered down. You can find different opinions on just about every player or game, so I try not to get affected by that stuff too much. It's more about just doing my own research and drawing my own conclusions so that I'm not biased one way or the other from something I read.

## How important is a routine to you?

A routine is *extremely* important for me, personally. I've made plenty of trips out to Vegas and L.A. and wherever to do the competitions for football, baseball, and basketball. I'm not using it as an excuse or anything, but it's extremely difficult for me to get out of my routine.

You go there and you might be on a different computer, you might be out doing stuff when you'd normally be in researching in your normal groove. For me, I really rely on that normal everyday routine. I have everything on my desktop computer and my play can suffer when I get away from it. That's something I really want to try to fix as I travel, but for guys who are on the road a lot, that's just an extra challenge thrown in there.

**Do you start your research with site salaries or wait to look at those?**

Yeah I don't look at the salaries until really late in the process. I start off by looking at the matchups, just trying to find guys who I like and don't like. I think that's most important in football, because if I really like a guy, I'll pretty much find a way to get him in there, and if I'm really down on a guy, it almost doesn't even matter what his salary is. The value and stuff is important, but it's more important to just figure out who is going to play well, who isn't, and then go from there.

**Which stats do you value most in the NFL?**

For quarterbacks, I actually prefer to look at numbers on the secondary before doing anything else. Quarterbacks are a little bit of a different breed, so I'm looking at secondary stats on Pro Football Focus and RotoGrinders. It's pretty easy to know which quarterbacks are best—it's not really hard to determine like it might be for another position—so I like to first look at the defense and grade the matchup.

For running backs, I like yards-per-carry. I know some people don't like that as much because it can get thrown off by long runs, but if a guy's YPC is inflated from long runs, that probably means he's explosive. And

YPC in general is generally a pretty good indicator of offensive line strength.

For receivers, the number one thing for me is touchdowns. There's certain types of players who score a lot, and particular players just get way more chances to score a lot. Scoring from 30 or 40 yards out is a fluky sort of thing, so red zone targets is probably the most important stat for me.

If you're seeing a ton of red zone looks, you're going to have a much higher chance of scoring, and that's gonna bump you up on my list quite a bit. Sometimes a receiver might be a little unlucky with how often he's converting those targets into touchdowns, but if it's a guy I know can score, I just care that he's getting the red zone looks and will keep getting 'em.

**How do you know when to trust the numbers and when to go with your gut?**

I'd say on the range of subjectivity, I'm definitely more of an instinct player than someone who sits down with a spreadsheet and tries to work out matchups and stats. I definitely understand that aspect of it and I consider those stats in my research, but that's not something that I personally do.

I think that ultimately you still need to have a feel for it and have some sort of instinct for it. I read a lot less expert stuff these days just because I think it can sort of cloud my own judgments. In the end, you need to figure it out for yourself.

One thing I'll say is that even though it's about trusting your instincts, that doesn't mean you can't improve your "gut" by using stats or other objective means. That stuff can help shape you as a player and help you make better decisions. But if you're just blindly following those numbers or listening to what a particular analyst says, that's not going to help much in the long run.

## How do you know when to trust or overlook player news? Do you use Twitter?

As far as player news, I really don't pay much attention to that stuff. The only thing I really care about is the injury stuff. If there's an injury concern, then I'll try to dig through that information and figure out what's likely to happen with him. You have to dig a lot sometimes because the reporters are wrong a lot, or else they're getting bad information because teams aren't that willing to disclose injury news.

But as far as generic player news like if a guy is expected to do well, I don't care about that stuff, man. Like I said, I really don't follow the analysis type of stuff. There are so many differing opinions out there that you can find whatever you want. And even in terms of injury stuff, I just want straight reporting instead of any type of predictions. The "this guy is battling through an injury" stuff isn't helpful to me. If you're healthy enough to be in the lineup, then I'm going to play you if you're ready to go.

In terms of Twitter, I really don't use it a whole lot for NFL stuff, to be honest. I don't even have anyone specific I follow for NFL news on there. That's more important for basketball and baseball.

**When doing research, are you looking more at a specific player/team, or do you care more about matchups?**

Well let me put it like this: in baseball, it's 99 percent matchup stuff. It's basically all matchup-based. In basketball, it's the opposite end of the spectrum; it's completely value-based. I know who the great players are in a given night, matchups don't matter as much, and I'm just looking to see how much value I can get out of you.

I think football is a mix of those two sports. You want the value in terms of the salary, you know, but you also need to consider the matchup. It's just a unique situation because neither one should be the only thing you consider, or even close.

Sometimes you can kind of disregard a poor matchup if the value is there, and other times a guy might have a juicy matchup and you might be a little more hesitant because of his salary. But you can't just load up on one or the other. If you're purely value-based, you might not have the best team just in terms of putting up a whole lot of points. Some guys might be poor values but can just go for 200 yards in any game.

If you're strictly matchup-based, you're ignoring a big part of puzzle. If we just stuck to matchups, everyone would have pretty much the same lineup. You can't just plug in a running back who's playing the worst run defense or something like that. But I've seen plenty of times when good offenses just explode on great defenses and not a lot of people used players from the game because it was considered a bad matchup.

Actually, that sort of thing happens every week in the NFL and a big part of playing daily fantasy football is figuring out when it's going to happen. If you can identify a situation where a team is going to maybe perform a little bit better than the matchup suggests or when a single player might bust out even though he doesn't appear to offer value, that's a big advantage.

So I care about matchups and value, but not to the extent that either one by itself defines who I'm going to play. It's a mix.

## CSURAM88's Analysis

Headchopper mentioned NFL Game Rewind and I really can't emphasize enough how useful that is for daily fantasy football. Thanks to NFL Game Rewind, I'm able to watch every play from every game every week. Football is a sport that can't be completely explained with data, at least not at this point, so there's value in studying the film.

The coaches' film is particularly useful because you can key in on certain players really easily—wide receivers or cornerbacks especially. I'm obviously still a data-driven player and I don't think there's a substitute for the analytics, but it helps to understand the foundation for those numbers, which watching tape can do.

There's also a ton of value in a daily routine, which headchopper touched on. For me, that means getting in leagues early so I don't have the stress of doing it all at the last minute, finishing all of the research that I can before injury reports come out, and so on. I like to monitor the activity of the Vegas lines, too. Doing all of that stuff at a set time is important; as you improve that process, you can really make it more efficient so that you can ultimately do more research and make better lineups.

A final thing that I want to note is that I actually create a lineup right after games have ended from the previous week. So on Monday night or Tuesday morning, I'll make a lineup before doing any sort of research—just my gut feel.

Once I do all of my research for the week, I come back to that lineup once the weekend rolls around and I look at what I initially liked about those players. When my research coincides with my gut, I'll definitely target those players. When it doesn't, I'll examine it more to see why I either liked a player who the numbers suggest isn't a good play, or why I didn't like a player who maybe I should have been on.

I don't simply trust my gut and I typically side with the numbers, but I think I can make good natural decisions and I have a decent feel for players and situations, so I always prefer my hunches to match up with the data. Making a lineup at the start of the week makes sure it's all about "feel" instead of being pulled one way or the other by the numbers.

## Jonathan's Analysis

Headchopper is one of the best NFL players out there, and he makes a lot of good points here. One of my favorite is that he searches for touchdown-scoring ability in receivers. Touchdowns are far less replaceable than yards and first downs, and we see the same type of receivers continually dominate near the goal line.

Here's a look at wide receiver and tight end red zone efficiency—the percentage of red zone targets converted into scores—broken down by weight.

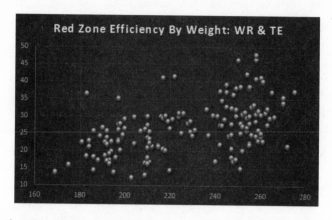

I've done more research on touchdown-scoring ability than anything else in fantasy football, and weight is the biggest predictor of touchdowns for receivers. It's actually amazing how closely the two are linked—even more so than height. NFL offenses continually undervalue the role of tight ends and big receivers near the goal line (even though they use them, it should be even more).

In terms of actionable advice, I think it makes sense to target receivers who are 1) going to see a lot of red zone targets and 2) likely to convert those into touchdowns. That's especially true in tournaments when you want as much upside as possible.

Slot receivers who see a high volume of targets can be useful in certain leagues on PPR sites, but they still don't possess elite upside if they can't score on a consistent basis. Ideally, your wide receivers should weight 210-plus (and preferably more) and have a history of red zone success.

## Chapter 2: Understanding Variance with C.D. Carter

C.D. Carter is the author of "How to Think Like a Daily Fantasy Winner" and, as I've come to learn through our interactions on Twitter, someone who really understands the role of variance in daily fantasy sports. C.D. spoke with poker pros to understand how people who excessive experience variance on a day-to-day basis not only deal with it, but also embrace it.

**Talk a little bit about your experience with variance and how it has shaped your outlook on fantasy football.**

I think avoidance of variance as a tool in fantasy comes with fear. Casual owners are fearful. Even many experienced fantasy owners are filled with fear of failing, of falling short, of whiffing on a player. It's as soon as you shed that fear, or at least some of it, that variance becomes your best friend.

Using variance requires a view of player, team, matchup, or offense that is outside the mainstream ,and that's not easy. It's painful, actually, and I do mean that in a literal sense. Taking a contrarian view—using statistical variance as a weapon—triggers the parts of our brain that control pain reactions. It hurts to use variance.

I used to be afraid of variance too, until I realized the long-term benefits of using variance in how I evaluate a player's fantasy prospects. It has changed the way I take chances—where I choose to take my shots—and I think I'm better for it.

## How do you think season-long variance differs from that in daily fantasy football?

Season-long variance, for one, requires a larger leap of faith for fantasy owners since you're going to be tied to these players for several months. That will probably make the use of variance unappealing for owners who want to leave their draft room feeling like they've created an indestructible team. This is very much anecdotal, I know, but the fantasy teams with which I've felt most uncomfortable after a draft are the very squads that win championships.

In daily fantasy tournaments, embracing variance is the only way to take home consistent cash. Like you've pointed out in your books, who cares if you finish 200th or 51st in a tournament if it's only the top 50 who take home money? Contrarianism and exploiting variance are the best ways to hit it big for low-stakes players who throw a few bucks into huge weekly fields.

## How would you compare the variance in poker to DFS?

I'd say variance is similar in poker and DFS in that bad breaks occur in both, whether we're talking about a streak of cold cards or in-game injuries, for example. Variance in both games is enough to make you lose your mind sometimes, though *a commitment to process over results* in poker and fantasy football will help anyone deal with the effects of variance, good and bad.

## Do you think variance makes games more or less beatable?

Philosophically, I want to say more beatable, and I think analysis of variance has shown that the mere existence of variance benefits those who recognize its power.

## Are there any specific ways you incorporate variance into your DFS strategies?

I try to find at least one guy or one QB/WR/TE stack that would make me very right or very wrong, all by my lonesome. In other words, I know I'll whiff, but when I'm right, the potential rewards are much greater than if

I were to have ignored variance as the centerpiece to a DFS strategy.

**How can a player know when his results might be due to swings in variance or actually the result of skill?**

I think it's impossible to know for sure without keeping some sort of notes about how you make your decisions in fantasy football. I interviewed Alan Schoonmaker—an esteemed author of poker psychology books—and he said note-taking changed his approach to poker. An unerring focus on process should be paramount for DFS players, but first understanding whether or not your process stinks is critically important.

## CSURAM88's Analysis

I think that poker is definitely a good comp for understanding variance in daily fantasy sports. One thing I'll mention is that, especially in regards to daily fantasy football, it can take a pretty long time to understand the variance in the game. There are so few games during the season, so there's really a lot more variance in football than other sports.

I'd say that the main difference between football and poker is that, whereas you can look back on a year of poker hands and figure out how to improve or what you're doing wrong, you might not be able to do that after a season or even a few seasons of daily fantasy football. That doesn't mean you can't win, though, because so many players treat the game as though there isn't that much variance, so just understanding variance in general can give you an advantage over the field.

Plus, variance makes the game beatable by anyone— any player can come in and find success right off the bat—which helps people stick around and helps the industry to grow. It's a good thing that there's a lot of variance.

In terms of gameplay, understanding variance is critical; you need to know that players have a certain range of potential outcomes, for example, and how likely they are to reach their ceiling, how likely they are to tank, etc. Selecting good tournament lineups is about knowing which players have the greatest likelihood of reaching their ceiling production, for example, which necessitates a comprehension of variance.

## Jonathan's Analysis

I think at the heart of understanding the value of variance in daily fantasy sports is the realization that everyone must deal with it. In a vacuum, variance seems detrimental because it hinders our ability to create optimal lineups or maximize projected points. Our goal isn't to maximize our projection, however, but rather to maximize our win probability. There's a difference between the two. C.D. alluded to playing lineups that are unpopular and although they might not hit often, they hit in a big way when they do. This is an antifragile approach to daily fantasy that attempts to benefit from chaos. What could go wrong, how would that affect most of the field, and how can I benefit?

Another huge idea here is that variance/randomness is unpredictable. I couldn't disagree more. Actually, I think random events can ironically be among the most predictable things in the world over large samples because we know that they're going to regress toward the mean.

Take the performance of an MLB hitter with a .300 career average, for example. In a given night, it's really hard to predict how he'll hit; he could go hitless or he could go 4-for-5. Over the course of an entire season, though, we know that he'll almost assuredly fall between .280 and .320.

In daily fantasy, you have a whole bunch of people who are playing the game as though there's no variance at all—like the results from each week in the NFL are the word of God or something. They'll play as though that crappy receiver coming off of a game with two touchdowns is going to score again the next week, and understanding how variance works can get you out of such situations.

Football isn't totally random by any means, but even if it were, you could still win playing daily fantasy because you're competing against others who are doing the equivalent of guessing heads because heads came up on four straight coin flips. If you're getting 2:1 odds on tails, you're going to win over the long run.

One final point I want to make about variance, particularly in the NFL, is that it can often lead you to players who appear to be "down." If past production were a perfect indicator of future production, we'd never want to target players in the midst of hot streaks. If football were pure randomness, it wouldn't matter who we target (or, more accurately, we'd just want to pay as little as possible for them).

Well, we're somewhere between those two extremes, so the more variance you believe is inherent to the game, the more you're going to fade "hot" players and jump on those on whom others are down, knowing their production—despite perhaps being filled with variance—will eventually regress toward the mean in a predictable manner. Plus, you can just get a good price on them, which is key.

## Chapter 3: The Vegas Lines with Mirage88

I'm a huge proponent of "stealing" research from Vegas by looking at their game lines, spreads, totals, prop bets, and so on. These are people who have millions of dollars on the line with each game, so creating an accurate line is important to them. It's not that we can't know that the Broncos are going to score a lot of points without looking to Vegas, but rather that the lines allow us to 1) quantify the effect and 2) do it in a really efficient way so we can spend precious research time elsewhere.

I spoke with Mirage88—one of daily fantasy's up-and-coming players—about his use of Vegas. Mirage88 is one of the smartest people I've spoken to about daily fantasy sports. He's also my favorite daily fantasy success story.

Within two weeks of learning about daily fantasy, Mirage88 qualified for a daily fantasy football championship and then won $25,000 just one month after that. A few months later, he went on a two-week heater that included a six-figure profit.

| Rankings | Mirage88 |
|---|---|
| Overall updates weekly on Thursday. | |
| Overall Ranking | 60th (43132.85) |
| TPOY Ranking | 12th (13057.00) |
| Monthly Grinder Leaderboard | 16th (2920.07) |
| NFL Grinder Leaderboard | 26th (13937.53) |
| MLB Grinder Leaderboard | 43rd (11142.31) |
| NBA Grinder Leaderboard | 1616th (727.69) |

Currently ranked in the top 30 in NFL and top 12 in TPOY, I'd argue that Mirage88 is one of the top 10 daily fantasy players in the world.

## First, talk to me about the Vegas lines and how they're created.

I think it's important to understand how the Vegas lines are created, which then aids us in figuring out how useful they are. There's a perception that Vegas sets lines solely to get 50/50 action on each side of the bet. And to some degree they probably want that in many situations since they'll guarantee themselves profit just from the juice (the commission they charge to play). But what happens is people will sometimes use that as a reason that Vegas shouldn't be used in projections, saying something like "Oh, they just care about whatever popular opinion might be and just getting in the middle of that."

The problem with that is that there are a lot of sharp bettors out there with a lot of money, so if Vegas indeed produces a line to equalize bets but it's weak, those sharps are just going to pound that bet and Vegas will be in a really poor situation in terms of expected value.

So the way I like to think about Vegas is that it's really where the most risk is in terms of projecting any player results—at least the most financial risk from one entity making projections, anyway. So if Vegas posts a poor

line—let's say they post a total that's way too low—
then all of a sudden anyone who can bet on that who is
relatively sharp will just start hitting the over, and Vegas
will realize that the bet isn't really balanced.

Vegas will compensate for that by moving the total up
to get more action on the under. That's fine, but then
there's this area in the middle which was over the initial
line but under the new line movement bet that's now a
really bad place for Vegas. If the game ends up in that
spot, they could theoretically lose a whole lot of bets to
sharps who bet the original over, but at the same time
lose late bets that came in on the under when the total
was higher.

Vegas doesn't want to put themselves in that position
where they can be arbitraged, so it's really important
for them to create an accurate line from the start. Even
if they don't guarantee a profit by getting equal money
on each side, they can limit their downside—their risk
of ruin—by making the line accurate. They really don't
want to be in a situation where they set a bad line that
moves a whole lot and they could potentially lose their
share on both sides of a bet.

So to be clear, Vegas needs to set accurate lines to not
only ensure that they get equal money on both sides,
which they will, but so that *actual results* fall on both
sides of the bet 50 percent of the time over the long run
as well. It's okay if they get 70 percent of action on one
side of a bet and 30 percent on the other if, over time,
the actual results are falling half over and half under—
meaning Vegas is setting accurate lines.

Ultimately, making accurate lines is just a safer way for Vegas to make money than trying to predict public opinion, especially when there are sharks out there who might not agree with public opinion. Vegas has a very clear financial incentive to make accurate lines, and they do. So that's my little rant on why we can trust the lines and why the idea that all Vegas wants is to balance bets is false.

## How do you personally use the lines in your daily fantasy projections?

I personally use the lines whenever there aren't time constraints. So if the lines come out a couple hours before a game, that's a little difficult to fit into a model to make projections and still be able to create lineups and all that. But any Vegas line that comes out early enough that I think relates to something that I'm trying to project gets put into my model.

In football, I'm usually looking at projected totals the most. The easiest way to use over/unders in football is to look at the total and the spread and calculate the projected total for each team. You can do that pretty easily on your own, but I go to RotoGrinders for that info to get it really quickly.

Once I have the total for each team, I look at some historical scoring rates—what percentage of scoring has typically gone to each position for certain teams. So let's say we're looking at the Packers and the Giants, who Vegas has projected at 24 points each. By looking at historical scoring, we'd see that we should project Aaron Rodgers with more touchdowns than Eli Manning just because Green Bay scores a higher percentage of touchdowns to field goals, and Rodgers also accounts for a much higher percentage of the Packers' scores than Manning for the Giants, even with the same projected points.

You need to be careful there, too, because there can be a lot of turnover in the NFL, so things change. For example, the Giants have a new offensive coordinator and an entirely new offensive philosophy, so that data on how their touchdowns are usually allocated might change. For the Packers, on the other hand, we can pretty much assume the same scoring rates since not much has changed for them in terms of coaching or personnel.

I think that's also a good example of projections sometimes being really scientific and other times being more of an art. With Green Bay, I'd be more likely to rely on the numbers; I can look back at however many years the same sort of scheme was in place and say, "Okay, 20 percent of touchdowns go to Jordy Nelson, 35 percent go to running backs, and so on."

You can actually do the same sort of thing when projecting kickers, looking at a combination of the line and then what percentage of points the kicker has produced, assuming there haven't been giant shifts in offensive philosophy or personnel.

After that, you still need to adjust for other factors, specifically the opponent. Maybe the Packers' wide receivers account for 50 percent of all touchdowns, but they're facing a defense that has really short cornerbacks who get picked on in the red zone, so they allow 65 percent of touchdowns to opposing receivers. Then you'd expect an even greater rate of the scoring to come from Nelson & Co.

But that's the general idea behind what I do to at least get a baseline projection.

### Do you study only totals? How about player props?

I don't use props, but not because they aren't useful. They have the same predictive power of any other number put out by Vegas. The main reason I don't use the props, though, is that they tend to come out pretty late in the week, so that doesn't leave much time to get them into my projection model. I can pretty much calculate projected touchdowns, especially, from using the total and past scoring rates alone, so I can do that earlier in the week when the lines are posted. That's a way to basically get most of the way to creating the props without the props actually being released.

The other thing is that I think there's something to be said for simplicity in a model. It's really important to understand everything that goes into your model and how it affects the projection, and sometimes it doesn't make sense to have all these little minute details coming in from 50 different sources.

So I don't know if I'd make player props a major component of my model even if they did come out earlier in the week, just because it's important to understand what's driving your model in order to improve it. If you have a bunch of different components in your model and it doesn't work, it's going to be really difficult for you to figure out why and make a change. A huge part of being a profitable daily fantasy player is about improvement, so you need to know where your projections are coming from and how they can be enhanced.

**What percentage of players do you think look at the lines? How does that affect their worth?**

I'd say that almost all high-volume players are looking at the lines in some form or another. Some put more weight into them than others, but if you're a successful daily fantasy player, I'd be surprised if you aren't looking at the lines at all.

In terms of the overall player pool, though, I think it's probably still a tiny percentage, which adds to their worth. I think there's a ton of value in using the lines, especially in cash games, because in head-to-head or 50/50 matchups, for example, you're just looking to figure out the most likely thing that's going to happen and use that to beat the average player. Using the Vegas lines is a really accurate way to accomplish that.

In cash games, I think Vegas can really help with your own projections. In tournaments, I think the biggest value from the lines comes in using them as a prediction market for ownership. So the higher the over/under on a game, the more player utilization there will be in those games. Even if the general public isn't using the Vegas lines, they still have a sense of which games are going to be high-scoring, so Vegas can act as confirmation of where there's going to be heavy player usage.

That's important because, unlike in cash games, it's important to have a unique lineup in tournaments. So if there's a game that's an outlier in terms of the projected total, just way ahead of everything else, it's kind of hard to recommend players from that game because they're going to be so popular. That doesn't mean I never use players from the highest-projected game in tournaments, but if I do, I need to create some elements within my roster that I think won't be as common elsewhere. It's not that you can't win by using all highly utilized players, but just that it can improve your tournament odds by adding at least some contrarian elements into your lineup when you otherwise go with the chalk.

## How do you know when to go against Vegas and when to play the chalk?

I think this is one of the aspects of daily fantasy that's still more art than science. My general philosophy, at least in tournaments, is to take the best possible players who I think won't be really popular choices for the rest of the daily fantasy community.

So let's say that the Broncos are projected way ahead of everyone else in a given week and also have some attractive salaries, to the point that we pretty much know Denver players are going to see extremely high usage. In that situation, I tend to look at the next few highest-projected teams and then try to think about which ones won't be very popular—maybe they aren't getting a lot of buzz or they play in a small market—and try to target players on those teams. Even if they aren't projected quite as high as the Broncos, you make up for that by creating a lineup that doesn't resemble many others, whereas maybe 30 percent of the field is creating very similar Broncos-centric lineups.

So in a way, I'm still playing chalk in that I want them to be projected to score a lot of points, but just that I care about how popular I think a team's players will be, too. It's also an experience sort of thing where you'll get better as you play in more tournaments.

Another time when I like to go against the top-projected team is when I see certain players on poor teams come out as really good values. Maybe there will be a case where a team isn't projected to score that many points, but their quarterback and top receiver are likely to account for a huge percentage of their overall yards and touchdowns. I love to target those situations because I can still get value with the projections, but I know the public won't be on them because they aren't projected that high as a team. So again, I'm just using the Vegas totals as a proxy for daily fantasy ownership.

## What percentage of your model is composed of Vegas-based data?

It depends on the sport. I think Vegas is a really powerful tool, but it's just one of many projections I use. One of my goals is to find as many projections from as many smart people as I can find and just aggregate them. So I make projections myself, I use Vegas, I look at sites that I trust, and I factor all of those into my model.

As long as I think the projections are coming via a quality process, I love to just aggregate a whole bunch of information to factor out as much bias as I can, whether it's my own personal biases or individual site bias. So Vegas might be just one-fourth or one-fifth of my model, although I do change the weight I place on each source as I see fit.

The bigger picture is that I really am a huge proponent of aggregating data from a few trusted sources. I think it's the easiest way to build an accurate projection—the "wisdom of the crowd"—and Vegas is a big component of that, although certainly not the only source I rely on.

### Which aspects of daily fantasy projections aren't priced into the Vegas lines?

For the most part, I think they're going to do a really good job of capturing most relevant statistics. Again, there's so much money on the line that it's hard to believe there's a really powerful predictive measure that they aren't considering.

But if something isn't priced in, it's factors that they aren't aware of when they set the line. The biggest example of that is weather. Vegas posts lines early in the week without full knowledge of weather conditions days down the line, so that's something that certainly affects player production but won't be a major component of the early lines. The classic example is a 2013 game between the Eagles and Lions that had a huge over/under that was posted on Monday—a total that needed to be adjusted considerably because forecasts were calling for a massive blizzard during the game.

It's not just Vegas that doesn't initially account for weather, though. Most projections aren't going to have weather as much of a component to start just because we can't really know how the weather is going to look during a game days in advance. So weather is a really, really important aspect of projections to monitor.

Injuries are another aspect of daily fantasy production that might not be priced into the Vegas lines when they first come out. Let's say Aaron Rodgers is questionable but expected to play in a given game, but just before kickoff he's ruled out. Vegas might have set the total as if Rodgers were going to play, but that's going to be altered significantly if he can't go, which will of course extend to projections for his teammates as well.

## Do you ever study line movements? How might those be useful?

I don't think the lines move all that much in most cases because, like I said, Vegas generally posts strong lines. When it does move a lot, I think that's really good evidence of strong public perception in one way or the other.

That has the most use in tournaments because if you see the public strongly moving in one direction, that should probably be a reason for you to move in the other. I think you want to avoid following the public when a line moves because basically that's a case where the general populace likes a team more than Vegas does. We can usually equate the general betting populace to the average daily fantasy player, so when a line moves a lot in a particular direction, it's a decent sign that a lot of users are going to be higher on certain players than Vegas would be—and thus their ownership will be higher than it should be.

Whether or not I target players in a game that moves a lot depends on which direction it moves. If a game moves up, it means that there's probably going to be heavy usage on players that Vegas doesn't like as much as the public, and that's a situation to fade. If a line moves down, though, it means Vegas is higher on a team that the public, and that's often a situation to target because you can get value on players who are unlikely to be heavily utilized. That's not a hard-and-fast rule that I use—again, it's still more of an art than science at this point—but it's a good rule-of-thumb regarding value and ownership percentages.

**Tell us about a time when you successfully leveraged Vegas.**

I have an example from MLB. After completing my baseball projections for the day, I ranked my top teams to stack simply by sorting average fantasy points per batter on each team. I saw that the Cubs were the sixth-highest total out of 20 teams in my model, but had the third-lowest projected total in Vegas. The downside of that over/under was already included as an input in my projection, so I felt good going with the Cubs despite the low projected total.

I also got a sense that the opposing pitcher, Tyler Lyons, was going to be highly owned based on industry articles and podcasts recommending him. Given that Lyons isn't an ace pitcher and my model had batters with a decent projection against him, it was a perfect opportunity. I got to stack a low-ownership team while getting double the value, as the poor performance of the opposing pitcher would sink a lot of my opponents' teams. Regardless of outcome, that's the type of shot I love taking in big tournaments, because when they work they win big. In that case, I had three Cubs stacks finish 1-2-3 due to the contrarian nature of the picks which almost no one else had.

## CSURAM88's Analysis

I'm a huge proponent of using the Vegas lines for information because they've proven to be so accurate, and Mirage88 did a great job of explaining why that's the case. One thing the lines allow me to do which is different from some other players is target teams over players.

That is, I look at the Vegas lines and use those to help me figure out which teams are going to be able to score a lot in a game. Then, I try to predict which players on that team are going to be the main beneficiaries of that. That's in opposition to some other daily fantasy players who start by looking at individual players.

Overall, though, I am 100 percent a Vegas-based daily fantasy player; I use the lines as a very strong foundation for my projections and lineups, and I don't think there's a more efficient and useful way to go about playing daily fantasy. In addition to game totals, I look at team totals, line movement, player props—anything I can get my hands on.

## Jonathan's Analysis

I've done a decent amount of research on the effect of Vegas in daily fantasy. My personal belief is that the lines are particularly useful for running backs. If we look at the relationship between projected over/unders and quarterback fantasy points, there's a weak relationship.

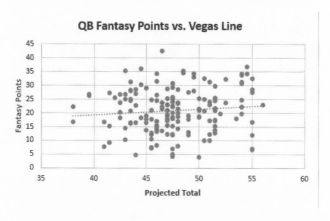

It strengthens a little if we look solely at projected team totals, which is obviously recommended, but it's still not nearly as strong as the relationship between projected points and rushing yards. Check this out.

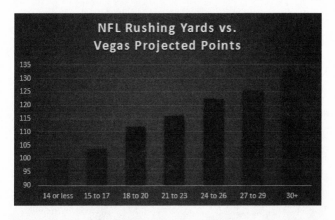

Teams projected to score 30 or more points in a game rush for around 14 percent more yards than those projected at 21 points and nearly 33 percent more than those at 14 or less.

So why are the Vegas lines a better proxy for rushing totals than passing? Think about game scripts. When NFL teams win, they normally do it because they pass the ball efficiently. It's not always the case, but frequently a team will pass the ball well, gain a lead, and then run out the clock. Meanwhile, the opponent probably didn't pass the ball very efficiently, faced a deficit, then made up for the poor passing efficiency with more late attempts.

Thus, passing stats often converge, with winners racking up fantasy points via efficiency and losers doing it with more attempts. On the flip side, rushing the ball is more correlated with winning than passing it. Note that I'm not saying rushing the ball often is a *cause* of winning; NFL coaches have made this mistake in the past (and still do), running the ball way too often because "hey, that's what teams that win do." Yeah, no shit, because they're *already winning*.

You can of course use Vegas props to project quarterbacks and receivers, too, and I also think the game location is important. Specifically, I like to target quarterbacks who are playing at home. Take a look at their passing efficiency over the years.

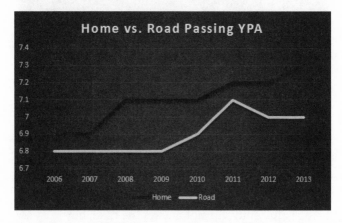

There are probably a lot of reasons for this effect, but ultimately there's a lot of value in targeting quarterbacks on home underdogs. First of all, they're likely to have greater efficiency than on the road. Second, they're probably going to throw the ball often as an underdog. Third, they're far less likely to be conservative early—something that coaches who are pussies still do on the road way too much—so you have the perfect storm of throwing the ball often *and* well.

## Chapter 4: Projecting Players with MrTuttle05 and Dinkpiece

There's no area where daily fantasy players want to improve more than in creating projections; if you can create accurate projections, you can make money playing daily fantasy sports. I spoke with two top-tier players in MrTuttle05 and Dinkpiece regarding their projection methodologies.

MrTuttle05 is the co-founder of FantasyInsiders.com and FantasyPros' 2013 Daily Fantasy Accuracy champ. He has qualified for the DFBC (three times), FFFC, DFFC, PFBC, and finished second in the PFFC. He's also currently ranked by RotoGrinders as one of the top 10 NFL players in the world.

| Rankings | MrTuttle05 |
|---|---|
| Overall updates weekly on Thursday. | |
| Overall Ranking | 15th (126715.80) |
| TPOY Ranking | 38th (7960.54) |
| Monthly Grinder Leaderboard | 91st (544.40) |
| NFL Grinder Leaderboard | 7th (33734.32) |
| MLB Grinder Leaderboard | 36th (12131.68) |
| NBA Grinder Leaderboard | 31st (28990.77) |

Dinkpiece founded MyFantasyFix.com and joined RotoExperts in 2013. That same year, he left his job as an investment analyst to play daily fantasy sports full-time, and his transition was featured by The Wall Street Journal. Dinkpiece was the 2012 Super Joust champ, along with a finalist in the DSFC, DSBBC, DSBC, PBC, and 2014 DraftKings Showcase.

Dinkpiece's ability to win across a variety of sports is amazing.

| Rankings | dinkpiece |
|---|---|
| Overall updates weekly on Thursday. | |
| Overall Ranking | 4th (293721.70) |
| TPOY Ranking | 7th (14512.46) |
| Monthly Grinder Leaderboard | 13th (2673.11) |
| NFL Grinder Leaderboard | 12th (25187.94) |
| MLB Grinder Leaderboard | 3rd (58033.28) |
| NBA Grinder Leaderboard | 3rd (142836.07) |

Currently ranked No. 7 in the RotoGrinders Tournament Player of the Year rankings and No. 4 overall, Dinkpiece is a top 12 NFL player.

## What are the general steps you take in projecting players? Is it more subjective or objective?

**MrTuttle05:** I'm probably a bit more subjective in regards to football research. I don't use a model or anything like that to project players. I look at some other data-driven projections from various sites because I think that can be helpful, but I don't usually do that until after I've performed my own research and figured out who I like on my own. I want my thoughts to be my own, so I tend to steer clear of that stuff until after I've picked a general pool of players that I'm going to target.

After I've decided who I like, I'll look at some others' stuff and then see where we agree and disagree. When I'm in agreement with others' work, that's kind of reassuring to me and lets me know that there are probably reasons to like a certain player. That doesn't mean I won't play someone who other people dislike, but just that there's value in a consensus opinion.

**Dinkpiece:** My research for NFL really starts with injuries. I'm looking at news throughout the week and waiting for the injury reports, so from that standpoint, it starts out qualitatively. I've run some numbers on players who are listed as 'questionable' or worse and still play. The numbers aren't overwhelming overall, but for certain positions, there are drops in production and so you really need to pay attention to the injury status. Even if a guy plays, you might want to fade him depending on his position and the injury.

The next step for me is far more data-driven. I start by looking at consensus rankings. FantasyPros is one of my favorite sites because you can find aggregate expert rankings, which is really useful. So that's just a great place to start to get an idea of how players should be ranked and projected.

The next thing I do is start to get a sense of opportunities. I look at various team-driven stats to see what type of run/pass balance I can expect from each team in every game. That includes not only their own run/pass balance, but also the run/pass balance allowed by the defense. Sometimes you have situations where a team runs the ball a lot, but mostly late in games, so if they're expected to be trailing, they probably won't be running as much as normal. But the opportunities are so important for fantasy football, so that's really where the majority of my research is directed—looking at how defenses are attacked, how teams like to beat them in the red zone, and so on.

Another thing to understand is how one particular aspect of a defense affects play-calling against them. Sometimes, certain defenses can be so good against the run, for example, that opposing offenses throw the ball a lot more than normal. That defense's actual passing defense might still be good, but they'll frequently give up decent passing numbers just because they get thrown on so much. If that's a team that gets passed on a lot in the red zone, too, I'll target quarterbacks/receivers against them, assuming I'm projecting a specific type of game script that will allow for favorable passing situations.

Ultimately, what I'm trying to do is use consensus rankings as a foundation and then alter those based on opportunities, which I think most players weight too lightly. That helps me create a projection for wide receiver targets, running back touches, and so on. For running backs, I look specifically at red zone carries; touchdowns are so important for backs and they're easier to project based on offensive philosophies and defensive weaknesses.

**Dinkpiece, you mentioned FantasyPros as a source for aggregate projections. Do you think certain people can beat a consensus of experts long-term?**

**Dinkpiece:** Yeah, I use the aggregate projections, but I also think certain people can indeed beat the consensus long-term. The reason is that there can sometimes be a herd mentality in expert projections and rankings that creates inefficiencies. So if 95 percent of experts aren't considering a factor that's actually quite important, that's a chance to beat the consensus.

However, I think the number of people who can actually beat the consensus is very low, and I also think you should approach projections as if you *can't* beat the consensus. I personally don't act as though I can beat FantasyPros' rankings on my own because that could actually put me at a disadvantage in terms of placing too much confidence in my projections. I use the aggregate to find areas where I might be overlooking a player, or just to see where the majority of people are headed in a given week in terms of player utilization.

**Which stats do you consider most when projecting for NFL?**

**MrTuttle05:** I think this is probably where I differ a lot from the typical daily fantasy football player. Basically, when I'm projecting NFL, I'm concerned less with finding a bunch of different stats and more with projecting opportunities. Obviously matchups matter in the NFL, so that's something to consider, but I really do that stuff secondary to figuring out how many chances players will have to make plays. That's really where fantasy points are scored; the matchups don't matter if a player doesn't get enough opportunities.

So the foundation of my research is looking at stats that are going to help me predict if a player will at least have the opportunity to produce. That means targets, red zone work, and stuff like that. For wide receivers, I'll look at both projected targets and a recent history of targets, as well as the percentage of his team's targets that he's going to see.

Then I can start to deduce a workload. If I think a team will pass the ball X times and a particular receiver will normally see 20 percent of those throws, I'd project him around X * 0.2 targets for that game. It's the same sort of deal with the other positions.

One of the reasons that I start with opportunity, in addition to it just being really important, is that it's also really predictable. I can try to project touchdowns, but those are really volatile from week to week. If I'm continually finding players with lots of opportunities to score touchdowns or otherwise make plays, then I'll eventually hit on those.

So basically I use opportunity stats to weed out players and find a core group who I think will have lots of chances to score in a given week. From there, I then move onto matchup stats—defense vs. position—to figure out which of those options is in the best spot to really do something with his touches.

**Dinkpiece:** Again, it all comes down to opportunity stats—targets, attempts, carries. There are a lot of really great rate stats out there, and while I consider those, they don't get too much weight in my projections. In the NFL, the samples are so small, so it's difficult to always trust those rate stats. What happens is that you often see a game or two really influencing the overall data too much. I'm more concerned with figuring out how many chances a player will have to score a lot of points and then using an adjusted baseline efficiency rate to finish the projection.

One rate stat that I do like to use is anything related to cornerback strength. I look at how well cornerbacks have played both historically and in the recent past. I get most of that data from Pro Football Focus, and it's just a good way to see who is struggling and which cornerbacks are being tested.

Another rate stat that I'll look at is the percentage of a team's workload a player receives, which is related back to opportunities. I look at the percentage of red zone targets each player receives, for example, as a way to determine who's most likely to get chances to score.

A final rate stat—again one related to opportunities—is the overall success rate of an offense. How often do they convert first downs and sustain long drives? I want efficient offenses just because they're more likely to stay on the field and run a lot of plays.

The game script is always important in predicting workload, too, so that's one area where I really focus. I look at the Vegas lines and just think about different ways a game could unfold; the score obviously has a huge effect on play-calling, so understanding and accurately predicting that is important. A lot of times, I'll target quarterbacks who are either going to be in a close game or even losing in the game (preferably a high-scoring one).

The final thing I want to say with opportunities, and this is kind of related to game scripts, is that I want to project not only the workload, but also the consistency of the workload. Some players have games where they'll see a huge workload and others when they barely see the ball. C.J. Spiller is a player like that who I might use in a tournament, but I'd never use him in a cash game just because you can't rely on him seeing a significant number of touches.

I know I'm harping on opportunities a lot, but it really is a huge thing. If you can do the research to add just a couple targets per receiver or a few carries per running back, that's going to do wonders for your daily fantasy success.

## How about projections kickers and defenses?

**Dinkpiece:** At kicker, I'm generally looking among the cheapest options because they're so volatile, but there's still some nuance to it. A lot of people say they look for the cheapest kicker on a high-scoring offense, but I don't want the offense to be too efficient or else they'll steal field goal opportunities.

I like to target kickers on teams with decent offenses but maybe those that aren't that efficient in the running game, specifically in short-yardage situations. Those teams tend to pass the ball more in the red zone, and passing produces binary outcomes down there; it's usually either a touchdown or not, which sets up longer third downs and can result in more field goal tries. If you can identify an offense that can move the ball up the field but might struggle punching it into the end zone, that's a good opportunity for points from short field goals.

For defenses, the main thing I look at is the opposing offense. I want defenses facing offenses that give up a lot of sacks, which usually results in a lot of turnovers. The defenses playing on heavy favorites are usually good plays because when they're playing from ahead, they get way more opportunities for sacks and takeaways against an offense that's dropping back to pass on every snap. The perfect storm for a defense is facing an offense that either wants to or must pass the ball a lot, but is inefficient in doing so.

The other way to pick a defense that I see more often in cash games is to go super-conservative with one in a game that's projected to be really slow-paced. I wouldn't recommend that strategy in tournaments because you want upside from sacks and takeaways, but targeting defenses in games projected to be slow-paced without a ton of plays—or a lot of running plays—is a safer option to limit downside. I tend to be more aggressive with my defense selection, however.

I tend to go pretty cheap with my defense, but that's not always the case. There are situations when I'll pay for a defense that's in a really good situation against a turnover-prone quarterback, but in general, I allocate a low percentage of the salary cap to my defense.

**How much variance do you think there is week to week? Do you place more importance on the player or the matchup?**

**MrTuttle05:** There's a good amount of variance each week in the NFL. In general, basketball is the most consistent sport on a nightly basis, so you can predict production there a lot easier. The players have lots of chances to get rewarded for their performance. It's not like that in football, so like I said, I'm just concerned with figuring out opportunities.

In doing that, I'm more concerned about the player than the matchup. The matchup matters, but it starts with making sure you're in a position to expose your lineup to lots of potential scoring. A player like Darren Sproles is an example of someone I don't normally roster. Even when he has a good matchup, his ceiling is limited, even in PPR leagues, because he rarely sees a heavy workload. So even against defenses with poor coverage linebackers who won't be able to keep up with Sproles, I'd be more likely to avoid him than the average daily fantasy player due to the lack of projected touches.

The only time I might go away from that a little is in tournaments just to go against the grain. Sometimes a player like C.J. Spiller can hit without a lot of touches, even if it isn't an optimal situation from an opportunity standpoint. In terms of my cash games, though, I wouldn't take a chance on a player like that.

**Dinkpiece:** This is a great question. I've done some research on how much the matchup matters at each position and, in general, the matchups matter *a lot*. When a player faces a bottom 10 defense, he has a 75 percent chance or more to outperform his normal production. That's a really high rate of success and suggests that the quality of the defense is probably just as important as the player in question.

The problem is really knowing how strong an actual matchup might be. Since there are such small samples in the NFL, you can get fooled into thinking that a defense is much better or worse than what's actually the case. For that reason, I think a lot of the defense vs. position stats aren't very useful until once we approach midseason. Before that, you're better off using a combination of this year's stats and last season's data. I personally just weight the defense less early in the season and focus more on player skill and opportunities. That's especially true if a defense has a lot of turnover in terms of personnel from one year to the next.

With respect to variance, there's a ton of it in football. It's very much like baseball in that a single play can make a player's day. A long fly-ball that gets held up in the wind and gets caught at the warning track can be the difference between winning a tournament or not, just as a single long touchdown can dramatically alter results.

The other thing that causes excess variance in the NFL is the injury risk. Throughout the course of the year, you'll have times when you have players leave the game because of injuries, and that's just not something you can predict. That adds a level of variance that the other sports don't have as much. It's important to try to account for that variance in your picks, especially knowing that it might not wear out over the course of such a short season.

## Do you do median projections or ceiling/floor?

**MrTuttle05:** I typically do a mental ceiling/floor projection. I think that has a lot more use than a median projection because you're typically concerned with either maximizing your floor or ceiling in a given week, depending on the league. So in cash games I want safe players and in tournaments I want guys with huge upside.

Lots of times the high-upside players also have high median projections, but that's not always the case; sometimes, you have players who are normally mediocre, but when they have a big game, it's *really* big. A median projection would probably lead you in the wrong direction in that case.

**Dinkpiece:** I know a lot of other good players approach it differently, but I tend to focus mostly on median projections because I play in a lot of cash games, so my concern is mostly on median value. When I enter large-field leagues, I obviously look more at ceiling projections, but the majority of my research gets placed into median projections.

### How much weight do you place on early-season results?

**MrTuttle05:** It really depends on the situation, but normally I don't place too much emphasis on the early data because it can just be misleading. You might have a player who has started the year on fire, but the stars aligned for him to do that. Or maybe you have a struggling stud who just hasn't gotten going because of matchups. Those matchups even out for the most part by the end of the year, but over the course of a few games, they can play a huge role.

I don't really care about the statistics, but I do look at other things like the roles guys are playing, how offenses/defenses are being run, how new coaches are calling plays, and so on. The beginning portion of the year is especially useful for players in new situations so you can get a feel for how they'll be used. That won't necessarily be reflected in bulk stats, but it's important to look at that stuff.

**Dinkpiece:** Like I said in regards to defenses, I don't place too much emphasis on early-season results. Over the course of just a few games, you'll see a lot of variance; maybe a defense looks good but just had three really easy matchups. I'll use some scouting services like PFF to help early in the year to try to decipher which teams/players are really playing well, but I mostly wait until around Week 7 or so to really start focusing on that data more heavily.

## How much do you use Vegas in your projections?

**MrTuttle05:** I don't use Vegas as much as some other players, but I use it a lot in accordance with weather. I'm not a meteorologist and I can't really predict how certain weather is going to affect scoring with much accuracy. I know which teams and players are the most likely to score the most in a given week, but I can't tell how much the wind is going to affect passing, for example.

So I look at the Vegas lines, especially right before the games when we have a really good sense of the weather, to see how the experts are projecting the conditions to affect scoring. If there's a lot of movement in one direction or the other before the game, that's important to me. There was a game in Chicago a year or two ago when the wind was just out of control, and the both the line and passing player props dropped considerably. That's an example of a situation when I'll be likely to lean on Vegas heavily.

**How much of a factor does weather play for you, Dinkpiece?**

**Dinkpiece:** I actually don't care that much about weather; I look at wind the most, and really just extreme wind conditions. I think people get scared away by rain or snow, but as long as there aren't heavy winds, I don't think an offense is really at a disadvantage. It could actually give them an advantage since they know where they're going on each play and the defense needs to react.

One time that precipitation might play a bigger role for me is if I think the offensive coordinator is going to change play-calling because of it. So if I like a receiver in a snow game but I think the team is going to run the ball way more and cut down on his opportunities, then I might stay away from him because of that.

I also consider weather for kickers. I don't want them in very cold or windy weather because the ball doesn't carry very far and teams are less likely to attempt field goals.

**What do you think are the advantages/disadvantages of a value-based projection system, such as $/point?**

**MrTuttle05:** Because of the volatility in NFL, I don't create a value threshold for each player that I'm looking to reach. That's something that's useful in basketball where the production is pretty consistent from night to night. In football or baseball, that's not the case and the values aren't as important.

It's not that the values are meaningless or can't help, but there's just so much variance that it isn't a great use of time. You can use up a lot of time creating values and then you might move down your value list quite a bit to select the players you like.

The other thing is that most $/point or value systems are based on median projections. Like I said, I'm more concerned with high/low projections for players—pure risk and reward—so the median values aren't that useful for me.

**Dinkpiece:** I don't follow $/point or other value systems religiously. I look at $/point just as I look at aggregate projections to create a baseline, but I think there's a problem with following values in a strict way because it's fragile.

Like I said, there's so much value in touchdowns or even long offensive plays in the NFL that they can totally change a player's game. You end up needing to project players very accurately—with fractional touchdowns, for example—to such a degree that you can't really be confident that the projections are right.

It's not that they have no value, but you can't blindly follow them because there is a really large margin for error. One defender falling down can totally change results, for example, and there's no way to accurately predict that.

I think the biggest value with $/point systems comes in identifying players who are obvious poor value. So I'll generally stick to players who come out near the top of the value systems or in the consensus projections, but I don't place so much emphasis on it that I'm always taking the top guys.

I prefer ranking systems. I sort players into tiers and then try to get as many high-tier players at each position as I can. I think that's the best course of action just because very specific projections place too much emphasis on fractional big events (touchdowns), and it's hard to evaluate those properly.

## Once you finish, how do you optimize your projections or rankings to create lineups?

**MrTuttle05:** The first thing I do is go onto the sites and look up player salaries. I already know who I think will do well in a given week, but I also want to know how much they cost on each site. That helps me not only identify undervalued players, but also know where they're the cheapest and where I should play them most in a given week. So if I like Dez Bryant and he costs 90 percent as much on one site as another, I'll of course try to get more exposure to him on the site where he's cheapest.

I cross-reference the names that stand out to me from a salary standpoint on each site with the players I have identified as guys to target from an on-field standpoint, and then I can get a sense of which players are going to offer value and where they're the most valuable.

**Dinkpiece:** "Optimize" is a buzz word for me; I don't really like it because I think it implies a level of precision that just doesn't exist. If you're going to be able to create a *true* optimal lineup, the projections need to be totally accurate, and again, I don't think that's possible.

I look through my tiers and compare the rankings with pricing to create the best lineups. I think that when you start to rely too heavily on $/point, you aren't putting your own stamp on your lineups; you're valuing the system over your own thoughts, which isn't always the best move.

I personally like to have a combination of both methods, using my own rankings alongside $/point and consensus projections. I think that's the best way to get the best of both worlds and create lineups that aren't so fragile as to blindly follow a projection system, but not totally subjective, either.

## CSURAM88's Analysis
Great thoughts here from two of the top players in the game. I think projections tie in with the previous two topics—variance and the lines. Like I said, Vegas should

be part of any projection model, but really understanding week-to-week variance can help you make better projections; people are so quick to overreact to results, especially in football because there's not much else to analyze. I think that's really the best way to get value in players, really—zigging when everyone else zags, jumping on players who people are down on (or those who have cheap salaries) because of factors that are just due to variance.

I also agree that daily fantasy players need to be careful when trying to translate their projections into lineups. Projections can be valuable, even if it's only because of the research you put in to complete them, but there's still a lot of subjectivity when trying to pick players from a list of values. There are so many players that there are naturally going to be a handful ranked very closely to one another, so you have to be able to pair players in an optimal way without just selecting the top values all the time.

## Jonathan's Analysis

Dinkpiece noted that he likes to look for pressure and sacks from his defenses, and that's a smart move. I've done a lot of research on this in the past, and it's amazing how strongly correlated pressure is with takeaways.

Over the last three years, teams that have ranked in the top 10 in quarterback pressures (via Pro Football Focus) have secured 39 percent more interceptions than those that ranked in the bottom 10 and forced 48 percent more fumbles. It's pretty incredible how well past pressure can predict future takeaways—much more so than even past takeaways.

By the way, I study pressures instead of sacks because the former is far more predictive. Defenses have historically sacked the quarterback on around one-fourth of all pressures. When you see a defense that starts the season with 20 sacks but only 30 pressures, they're almost assuredly going to see a major drop in their future sack rate. If you want to predict a defense's sacks per game, look at their pressures per game and divide that number by four.

Also, I prefer to analyze forced fumbles over fumble recoveries because the latter stat can be very volatile; once the ball hits the ground, it's very random as to who will recover it. When a defense recovers, say, 80 percent of the fumbles they force in a year, that's a really good sign they're going to recover fewer fumbles in the following season, for example.

Both players also brought up the wind. I looked into the effect of wind in my last book "Fantasy Football (and Baseball) for Smart People." Here's a look at how it alters passing efficiency.

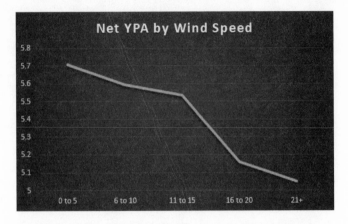

As Dinkpiece presumed, there's a big drop in passing success with strong winds; once you get above around 15mph, you're getting into the territory where it's going to have an impact on the passing game (and kicking game). In the typical game with winds in the 16-20mph range, a quarterback will be around 11 percent less efficient than he is inside of a dome with the conditions otherwise the same. That's going to have an effect on your projections.

Note that there's also an effect on play-calling; coaches adjust for the conditions and call fewer passes when it's windy.

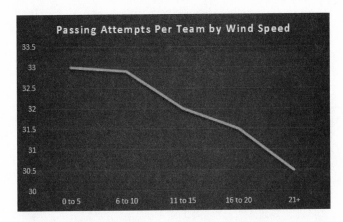

Combine this with the efficiency and you're looking at a dip of at least 15 percent in total expected production for the typical quarterback in winds of 16+ mph.

And in case you're interested in the effect of temperature on passing efficiency. . .

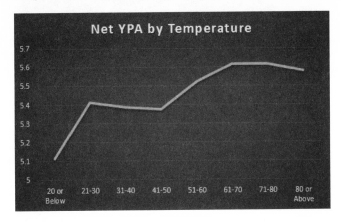

## Chapter 5: Winning Cash Games
## with PrimeTime420

Primarily a cash-game specialist, PrimeTime420 is currently ranked by RotoGrinders as the No. 7 overall daily fantasy player in the world. He's one of the premiere "jack-of-all-trades" players, ranked in the top 10 in NFL, MLB, NBA, and TPOY.

| Rankings | PrimeTime420 |
|---|---|
| Overall updates weekly on Thursday. | |
| Overall Ranking | 7th (222959.06) |
| TPOY Ranking | 5th (16828.68) |
| Monthly Grinder Leaderboard | 15th (5652.11) |
| NFL Grinder Leaderboard | 10th (30687.82) |
| MLB Grinder Leaderboard | 9th (38476.10) |
| NBA Grinder Leaderboard | 8th (74276.41) |

PrimeTime420's biggest week of NFL involved more than $90,000 in profit. He's been in more than 10 championship events, and he also earned an unbelievable 51 tickets into DraftKings' 2013 Millionaire Grand Final; with each ticket valued at $1,500, PrimeTime420 had $76,500 in equity in a single tournament. Still, cash games are the backbone of PrimeTime420's daily fantasy league selection.

**First, what do you define as 'cash games'?**

I define cash games as head-to-heads, 50/50s, or matrix games. I approach them with the same strategy, which is to play it safe.

**Talk about your head-to-head strategy. Is it all about maximizing your team's floor? Do you care more about safety or median projections?**

I tend to take the safe approach when it comes to my head-to-head strategy. I like to balance my whole team out, so yes, it is definitely about maximizing each player's floor for me. I don't like to spend too much cap on one position and hope those guys go off. I like to get guys who will do a solid job at each position and have very high floors.

That doesn't always give me the monster scores but it brings in consistent scores, which is what you are looking for in cash games. It also doesn't mean that I *can't* throw up a monster score, too.

For NFL, I spend very little on my kicker and defense, so that allows me to get higher-priced players who have the opportunity to go off. I prefer high-floor guys who also have high ceilings if that makes sense; I emphasize the floor, then look for players with upside, too.

## How many cash game lineups do you play in a given week?

I play one lineup on each site per week. I believe that is the best way to maximize your profit in the long run. Every once in a while, if I am having a hard time deciding on players, I will make small hedges and play two teams. Otherwise, I think the best way to truly optimize your profitability is to play a single lineup.

## How does DraftKings' PPR scoring affect how you approach your cash games?

Getting a full point per reception definitely affects my approach. My goal is to have as many receptions as possible on DraftKings, so I obviously target pass-catching backs rather than between-the-tackles, smash-mouth runners.

For receivers, I look for guys who are target monsters rather than red zone threats. I always want players who can score, but the targets really matter. I like to look for receivers who are on teams expected to lose, but facing a weak pass defense; those teams are likely to throw early and often, so the receivers usually get a lot of targets.

I also tend to avoid players on teams like the Saints who spread the ball around a lot. They might have a high projected total in a game, but the fantasy points are spread out so evenly that there isn't much upside there.

**How do you handle the flex in cash games? Is it flexible, or do you always play a certain position? Is your flex approach in cash games different from that in GPPs?**

On DraftKings, I play a running back in the flex almost every week in my cash games. Not any running backs, though—pass-catching backs. First of all, you are pretty much getting two players for the price of one. Guys like Jamaal Charles and LeSean McCoy can get just as many pass-catching opportunities as top-tier receivers some weeks.

On top of the receiving opportunities, the running backs also get their normal amount of carries and goal-line touches. With so many more chances to touch the ball, I think it makes the flex running back so much safer than other positions. And when I'm playing cash games, I will take the safe running back points over the high-risk/high-reward receiver any day.

With GPPs, however, I'm very flexible with the flex position. I try to swing for the fences and get that massive score, so going the safe route in tournaments is not the smartest thing to do. Sure, you might cash in the tournament, but you sure as hell won't win playing it safe.

So with the tournaments, I tend to go for the high-risk wide receiver plays. Sometimes I'll even throw the second-best tight end in the flex spot. I like to do that not only because they have touchdown upside, but also because it helps create a unique lineup in tournaments; few people play two tight ends.

The flex is also good for stacking. If an NFL team has a high total, I might play up to four skill players from that team, and the extra flex spot allows me to do that. There are times when I played Peyton Manning, Demaryius Thomas, Eric Decker, and Julius Thomas together in 2013, and that worked out a lot.

### How do you go about selecting your cash games? Do you try to handpick opponents?

On DraftKings, I pretty much get into any 50/50 league from $200 and down. I think I'm one of the best NFL players, so I'll hop into pretty much any game. Then I'll just post my head-to-head games rather than sniping games out of the lobby.

For one, DraftKings has a head-to-head blocker, so a lot of my action gets taken away from me by blocks. I can try to handpick players, but a lot of them won't work out, so I normally just need to wait for other users to accept my games anyway. Otherwise, if I feel like I don't have enough action, I'll just scoop up as many head-to-head games as I can before contests lock, regardless of the opponent.

However, if I were new to daily fantasy or if I had a smaller bankroll, I wouldn't pick games in that way. I would search head-to-heads and 50/50 leagues and try to avoid the best players as much as possible. I'd also spend as much time as I could sniping games from players I know are worse than me (or else new to the site). I would also play more of the multi-match games, as that can help offset bad nights while also giving you a diverse collection of opponents.

## What percentage of your total bankroll do you put into cash games each week?

For NFL, I play no more than seven percent of my bankroll each week. I'm a cautious player and I'm almost always in the range of five to seven percent, but I'd still never recommend more than 10 percent. Daily fantasy football can be so cruel when losing streaks are happening. You can go months without winning. So if you are playing a high percent of your bankroll, it can add up to big losses quickly if you don't scale back. However, if I'm up big early in the year and have a little "free money" that I can play around with, I'll take a few more chances.

### What's your typical allocation of funds for cash games?

Most of my games used to be head-to-head. Then DraftKings started to focus on the big 50/50 contests and I moved most of my action to those contests, simply due to a lot of players being there. I'd say about 75 percent what I spend each week goes towards both head-to-head and 50/50s, though, while the rest is focused on GPPs and qualifiers.

It changes from week to week, though. Sometimes, 90 percent or more will go toward cash games. The only time I have a lot of money allocated to tournaments is when a huge GPP is running, like the DraftKings Millionaire last year or something like that. Otherwise, I think the GPPs are too risky to play them as a primary source of income. By playing 25 percent or less of the money I spend in a given week in tournaments, it still allows me to make money even if I whiff on the GPPs.

### What traits do you value in each NFL position in cash games? Discuss your position-specific approach to cash games.

At quarterback, I don't like to discriminate. I love to use dual-threat quarterbacks as well as the traditional gunslingers. It all depends on the price and what kind of matchup they have.

If I think a running quarterback's team will be playing from behind, I love to play those guys. They'll have to make big plays to try and get back into the game, and a lot the time that translates into big runs. Add that to the normal passing stats and you pretty much get two players for the price of one.

However, most of the time I'll use a traditional quarterback because they're more consistent and less likely to have a *really* bad game. I'm sure there were people last year (like CSURAM88) who used Peyton Manning every week, and they were rewarded quite handsomely. So for me, it can be either a dual-threat quarterback like Kaepernick, Newton, or Wilson, or it can be the traditional passers like Manning, Stafford, or Rivers.

Also, Vegas is a huge deciding factor for me as well. I like to check out quarterback props to see who has the highest projected attempts, yards, and touchdowns. When all else fails, go with the guy who Vegas thinks will throw for the most yards and touchdowns.

At running back, I look for a lot of things. One is that I like to take backs on teams that are heavily favored. If a team is up early, they tend to pound the ball the rest of the game for some ball control.

As I mentioned, I really favor pass-catching running backs on DraftKings. When you can get backs who also see goal-line carries in addition to catching passes, like Charles, that's serious upside. Ideally, I'd like to find all three traits; if a running back is on a big favorite, catches passes, and sees goal-line work, that pretty much makes him a lock for me.

I also look for cheap backups when star running backs go down. There's a lot of turnover at the position with injuries, so those backups can be really valuable, especially if the injury occurs after site salaries are already set.

I also examine the opposition's run defense. I don't specifically target backs against a weak run defense, but I look at the run defense strength when deciding between backs who I like.

The main thing I want to avoid is timeshare situations; I don't want running backs who split carries. That's a pretty popular trend around the NFL, but I'd rather have a mediocre back who is going to get the majority of his team's carries than one who might be really talented but will see only 10 touches or something like that. The opportunities to score points matter a lot—even more than the talent level for running backs.

At the wide receiver position, it's all about targets. I want players like Pierre Garcon on DraftKings who I know are going to see a ton of targets and catch a lot of passes. I'll emphasize those guys over someone like Marques Colston, who might have a lot of touchdown potential but doesn't consistently see a huge number of targets. That's mainly true in my cash games when I'm looking for safety. Players like Garcon are really safe from week to week.

In tournaments, a lot of my wide receiver strategy centers around who I like at quarterback because I want to pair teammates. So if I like Stafford in a given week, I'll also clearly be targeting Calvin Johnson in GPPs. But using those pairs is something I do solely in tournaments; I almost never pair a quarterback and receiver in cash games because it's just too risky. The only exception for me has been Peyton Manning and one of his wide receivers because he's so good and has such a high floor each week.

Like with quarterbacks, I use Vegas when choosing wide receivers. Looking at props is a great way to determine who really has the best matchups of the week. Some guys' props are just too high to ignore, and they often turn into must-plays for me just based off of the prop alone. If there's one source that I'm going to trust and use confidently, it's the Vegas lines and props.

At tight end, I pretty much take it week by week. I'll first look at the top tight ends to see what their matchups are like. If Jimmy Graham or Rob Gronkowski has a quality matchup, then they're almost must-plays for me.

If not, I need to do more digging. I like players on high-powered offenses—Graham, Gronk, Julius Thomas, Vernon Davis—because they see more looks and become much safer bets. The tight ends on a lot of teams aren't used that much because there aren't enough targets to go around, so they become really risky each week, which isn't what I'm looking for in cash games. I'd rather overpay for someone like Graham who I know will see a high floor of targets. If you can hit on that, that's a huge advantage. It's also not as risky as doing it with other players because the cost is minimal and you still have a lot of cap space left over. So even if I pair a bargain bin tight end with his quarterback and they don't hook up for a touchdown, I can still make up for it with stud running backs and wide receivers.

The low-priced tight ends that I target are usually those who come into the game near the end zone—guys like Joseph Fauria and Ladarius Green. They're on high-powered offenses and can give you points even without a lot of targets, which is okay given how little they cost. They're risky in that they might not give you anything, but they also don't need to score a lot to return value.

## How do you tackle defense and kicker? Do you always go min-priced or near it?

I take the cheapest kicker or close to it nearly every time. I honestly hate kickers and wish all fantasy sites would take them out of the equation. However, if a few changes were made to the kicker scoring to make it more skillful I would be on board. For one, I believe a kicker should be penalized for a missed field goal. It's like a fumble or interception to me. It's a negative play for the team and they should get points taken away.

I also think that a field goal should be worth whatever the yardage is. So if a kicker connects on a 54-yard field goal, you would get 5.4 points. The fractional scoring would also help to break up some ties with the fractional points. But due to the variance at the position, especially with the current scoring, I don't pay up for kickers.

With defenses, it really depends on the week. Most times, I try to find one the cheapest defenses on the board with the easiest matchup according to Vegas. One of the first things I look at early in the week are the team totals. So if Vegas, who is right most of the time, thinks a team won't score much, I'll pounce on the opposing defense. I also look for defenses playing backup quarterbacks, which obviously can help lead to turnovers. I want defenses that can consistently get to the quarterback—and then defenses playing quarterbacks who will make mistakes once they're there.

The other thing I look for is a defense on a team that's the favorite. When a team is a big favorite, the opponent is often throwing late to catch up. Most of a defense's fantasy points come against the pass on interceptions, sacks, and fumbles, so I want defenses that are going to be getting thrown on a lot. Also, because that defense is *prepared* to be thrown on, it really helps them force turnovers and score touchdowns.

**How would you recommend that a novice start playing cash games?**

My first piece of advice is to take advantage of the beginner-only games on DraftKings. Those are the perfect way to get your feet wet and play with guys who are new to this as well.

The second piece of advice is to try to find a large-field 50/50 with as many top-level players in it as you can, but at a very low dollar level. Some top players will be in the $1 and $2 50/50s from time to time. If you enter those, you can study each roster from the top players to see what they are all doing the same and what separates the good players from great players. I still do that to this day to see what top players are thinking when I am feeling off or have been slumping.

The last piece of advice is to practice very strict bankroll management while still learning the game. I've seen too many players come in right away and get hot. Then weeks later they are never heard from because they got cocky and started playing too much of their bankroll each night. Even if you have a small bankroll, it's still important to learn the nuances of bankroll management so you can stay in the game.

## CSURAM88's Analysis

I think it's interesting that PrimeTime420 plays one cash game lineup per site each week. There's some debate about which strategy is best when it comes to the optimal quantity of lineups. I typically play more than one, but they're usually pretty similar, so it's not all that different of a strategy. I have one optimal lineup, then I typically submit small variations just to act as a little bit of a hedge. It's a risk-minimization strategy and I certainly don't recommend playing a bunch of lineups with all different players in your cash games.

In terms of picking opponents, I don't handpick anyone. I won't necessarily enter a league if I see that there are only sharks in it—I don't want to continually get matched up with the best players—but I don't seek out weak players. I'm profitable without doing that, so I try to do my best to do what's best for the industry, and having new players come in and have some success is definitely part of that.

As far as the flex position, I almost always use a wide receiver on DraftKings. There are really two schools of thought on the subject. I think wide receiver is definitely the play in tournaments for upside, and I think running back comes into play in cash games if you're looking solely for safety.

For me, I think I can find both safety and increase my ceiling a little more with a wide receiver in the flex on a PPR site like DraftKings, though, so that's usually the direction I head, regardless of the league type. I'm not against pass-catching running backs in the flex in cash games, though, and I still do that from time to time. It's of course all price-dependent; I won't force a wide receiver in there if there's a really cheap pass-catching running back who is better value.

## Jonathan's Analysis

One of my favorite aspects of daily fantasy football play is how to handle the flex spot. I think that's the biggest area where an experienced user can gain an edge over a novice, especially on a PPR site like DraftKings, because there are so many different ways to go with the flex spot. It's the only place where you need to make direct comparisons among players at different positions, which creates an entirely new layer of strategy.

PrimeTime420 mentioned he generally plays a pass-catching back in the flex in cash games and a wide receiver in the flex in tournaments. That's a smart decision according to the data.

In my last book *Fantasy Football (and Baseball) for Smart People*, I received data from DraftKings on what strategies are actually winning daily fantasy leagues. Here's a look at the probability of winning a head-to-head matchup based on which position is in the flex.

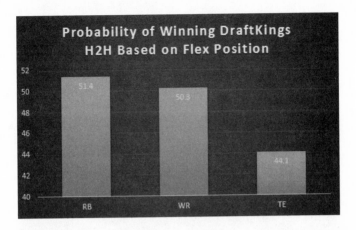

It's pretty remarkable that there's been so little success for tight ends as flex plays in cash games, but it makes sense; tight ends see the lightest workloads of any skill position, so they're bound to have the most variance from week to week. Wide receiver workloads are bigger, while running backs are a step above both.

You can enhance your cash game win probability by playing a running back in the flex, and specifically a pass-catching running back. Those players are extremely safe from week to week because they aren't reliant on a particular game path for points; they can contribute regardless of the score, and there's safety in that. They also see the most touches, meaning their play has the most chances to regress toward the mean, i.e. you get what you pay for.

If nothing else, the above data is evidence that a safe approach to cash games is indeed the correct way to approach them. That means projecting players' floors, asking yourself "What's the worst-case scenario for this player?" For running backs, that "worst case" is typically better than for receivers.

In comparison, here's a look at GPP win probability based on flex strategy.

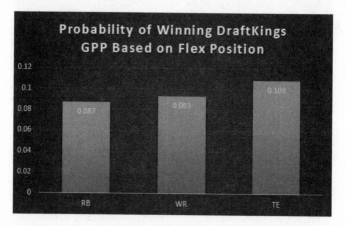

It's the exact opposite, which is even more evidence that safety wins cash games, while volatility wins tournaments. A running back might give you a high floor of points in a given week, but all except the truly elite backs don't possess ceilings as high as wide receivers on PPR sites like DraftKings.

Note that most tight ends' ceilings aren't quite as high as the top running backs, but they're also typically much cheaper, too. That means that playing a tight end in the flex 1) gives you a high ceiling *relative to the cost* and 2) allows you to spend big elsewhere.

# Chapter 6: Advanced Tournament Play with Al_Smizzle

Chicks dig the long ball, and in daily fantasy sports, GPPs are just that. Al_Smizzle knows what it's like to win $350,000 in a single daily fantasy football tournament, as he finished second in the 2013 DraftKings Millionaire. He's widely considered one of the best tournament players in the world.

| Rankings | Al_Smizzle |
|---|---|
| Overall updates weekly on Thursday. | |
| Overall Ranking | 13th (132522.90) |
| TPOY Ranking | 8th (14675.36) |
| Monthly Grinder Leaderboard | 54th (1718.57) |
| NFL Grinder Leaderboard | 18th (17915.82) |
| MLB Grinder Leaderboard | 19th (17534.54) |
| NBA Grinder Leaderboard | 9th (63053.71) |

I spoke with "Smizz" about general tournament strategies and his approach to taking down daily fantasy football GPPs on DraftKings.

**With the variance in tournaments, what percentage of your action (and your total bankroll) goes to GPPs?**

It really depends on the day/week and the type of tournaments, but the most of my bankroll I'll ever really play at once is 10 percent. That's not just tournaments;

that's money in play in all league types at one given time.

Then, I'll typically put about 80 to 90 percent of that into cash games—head-to-head, 50/50s, and so on. I actually prefer 50/50s the most just because there's some upside there too. But if you do the math, that's no more than 20 percent of my money that's in play in tournaments, GPPs, qualifiers, large-field leagues—whatever you want to call them—and just 10 percent of my money in play at once, max, which equates to no more than two percent of my entire bankroll being used for tournaments at any given time.

Some people are going to argue that I could be more aggressive, but I don't really think so, nor do I want to be. First of all, you can go on some pretty long cold streaks playing tournaments, and second, I chase a lot of qualifiers, which have the lowest short-term expected return since they're typically top-heavy and often award tickets instead of cash.

And again, that's a max—10 percent of the total bankroll in all games, two percent of the total bankroll in tournaments on any given day.

### What's your process for creating your tournament lineups?

Well, I start with my cash game lineup. I usually play just one cash lineup per site. So on DraftKings, I'll make one lineup for head-to-head and 50/50 games that I like, and then I tend to build my tournament lineups around the core guys that I like from that lineup.

You want different traits in tournaments, for sure, but you still want exposure to the best values, which you're playing in your cash games. And few guys who have a high floor that you might play in a head-to-head also have a really low ceiling so that you wouldn't want to use them in a GPP.

I use that foundation in most tournament lineups, then I fill in based on the type of tournament. In a qualifier, you basically want to win the entire thing, depending how it's structured, so I want as much upside as possible. In that format, I'm looking for high-ceiling players, and I'll also be more likely to use a contrarian strategy. I'm really looking to finish first, even if it means that a large percentage of the time I'll have a really poor lineup.

In typical cash GPPs, the first thing I'm looking to do is cash. I want to use the core values that I've found to cash, then just hope that those guys can hit enough to also propel me up toward the top. But it's more about value and a combination of safety/upside for normal GPPs, whereas in qualifiers I want all upside.

Also, I map out a certain budget at the beginning of the year that I have set aside just for qualifiers. So a lot of my qualifier strategy—at least the number I enter—is dictated by that budget.

**You mentioned being contrarian. Talk about that strategy and how much you use it.**

Being contrarian means purposely going against the grain so that you can have a unique lineup, which can help win a tournament. Like I said, my main goal in most GPPs—the first thing I need to do—is just to cash. So in that regard, I'm more of a value-based player than some other guys, so I just want pure value, regardless of ownership percentage. It doesn't matter to me if a player will be heavily utilized if he's the best value in a GPP. In qualifiers, I'm more contrarian-prone.

I don't mind going contrarian, but only if there's value there. I played Marvin Jones all over the place during his four-touchdown week in 2013, and he was like two percent owned (and I probably accounted for about half of that two percent in some tournaments). I didn't just play him because I thought others wouldn't, though; he had been getting more and more snaps and targets in the prior week, and I wanted to go high-priced at running back that week, so he just worked.

My strategy also changes a lot throughout the season. In the beginning of the year, I'm much more likely to be contrarian because everyone is basically picking players based off of season-long ADP, which is mostly based off of the prior season's stats. Football is such a unique sport in that the data from the previous year isn't really that meaningful, though; situations change, coaches change, personnel changes, so there aren't necessarily great numbers to use to determine team or player strength.

For that reason, I'm not as value-based early in the year just because it's more difficult to determine value. Then, I think there's a lot more value in going against the grain. As the season progresses, we get more and more data and we can see how certain players perform together or how coaches are calling things. By the end of the year, I care less about projected ownership because I think I can create more accurate values.

## Do you normally go against the grain on low-priced options like Jones?

No, not necessarily. One thing I really like to do is pay up for high-priced studs who maybe don't have an ideal matchup. When you have a player like Calvin Johnson, it really doesn't matter who he's facing; he can go for 200 yards against anyone. But if he has a bad matchup against the Ravens or something, you'll see his usage plummet.

Sometimes you'll have studs who are in only five percent of lineups because of the matchup, and that's a great situation. You get an elite player and you get to be contrarian at the same time. With those guys, the price and value don't matter as much because they have so much upside no matter what.

In my head-to-head games, I'm searching for the players who have the most access to a realistic outcome—an attainable threshold of production. In tournaments, I want players who have the most access to elite outcomes, and players like Johnson, Jamaal Charles, and so on can have those games against any opponent.

## How much does overlay matter to you?

It matters. I look at it, but I'm not going to go crazy chasing it. Some guys go way over their budget when they see overlay and it can end up killing them. It's not like you're just automatically going to cash when there's overlay. Even if a league fills up to only 80 percent, you're still going to see just 1-in-4 entrants cash, at the most, in the majority of tournaments.

I'll throw a couple extra lineups into a league when I see overlay because it's still a good situation, but you can't go over your budget. It more just changes how I structure my league selection; I'd be more inclined to place a higher percentage of my money into that league as opposed to putting extra money in on top of what I usually play.

Also, I consider overlay anything under the breakeven point for the site. Some people think that there's overlay if a 3,000-man tournament fills to only 2,900 entrants, but the site is still making money at that point, so you're –EV (negative expected value) as an average player. Overlay is actually anything where the site is losing money on the league.

## How do you structure your lineups with multi-entry? How much do you diversify?

It depends on the week, but I definitely diversify more than football than the other sports, particularly basketball. Football is really an event-based sport; the majority of the points come from basically one event—a touchdown—which can be really volatile from week to week. It's just difficult to predict who is going to score and how much, so that opens up the player pool a little bit.

I usually pick my core stacks that I like—usually one quarterback and one wide receiver—and then I build around those. I'll start with some players I use in my cash games, but I'll expand the player pool a bit. But it's not like I'm just picking everyone; it's about picking those core stacks and then building different player combinations around those.

That helps to make sure I actually cash if the stack hits. If I play a particular quarterback/wide receiver combination just once and they go off but the rest of the lineup around them doesn't do much, then I can't realize the potential of the stack. If I diversify more around that stack, I'll make sure that I hit with at least one of the combinations so that the stack doesn't get wasted, so to speak.

**Discuss your stacking strategy and how you mix and match players.**

Well, I'm almost always looking to pair a quarterback with at least one of his pass-catchers in a tournament. There's just so much upside to that strategy that you almost can't not do it. Sometimes I'll use a quarterback and two of his wide receivers or a wide receiver and tight end, but it depends on the team. That's a good strategy on high-scoring offenses like the Broncos; in 2013, we went into games pretty much knowing the Broncos would score four touchdowns, so there lots of upside in using the quarterback and two of his receivers. That's not the case on other teams.

Another type of stack that I like—and it isn't really a stack as much of just an optimal pairing—is using a running back and his defense. A lot of people overlook that, but a running back's play is correlated with the defense; if the defense does well, it probably means the team is winning, which will result in more late carries for the running back. That's a smart pairing that isn't that popular.

Another pairing that I like is a defense and kicker, particularly in games projected to be close and low-scoring. Lots of times, we'll see defensive battles where a team's defense is winning the field position battle and providing great opportunities to the offense, but they can't punch it in and need to settle for field goals. In those situations, you'll see a high correlation between defensive points and field goals. A lot of players want to start kickers on great offenses, but if they score a bunch of touchdowns, those field goal opportunities can disappear, i.e. the Saints.

## How about QB-RB-WR? Is there ever a good time to use that trio?

I wouldn't say that I never use a quarterback with his wide receiver and running back, but it's not common. It really depends on the situation; I might do it with Matt Forte or someone like that who can catch a lot of passes so that his play is correlated to the quarterback. But if a running back can't catch passes and score on those receptions, it's tough to get him in there in a stack.

It's kind of like using a hitter against the opposing pitcher in baseball. It's not impossible that the pitcher and hitter both have a great game, but it's not likely because their production is inversely correlated. In most cases, you just wouldn't be playing the percentages. It's not that it *can't* work, just that it isn't optimal.

## How does the PPR format on a site like DraftKings affect your GPP approach?

Oh man, it really changes how I build a lineup. Even the difference between full PPR and 0.5 PPR is huge. I think it's obvious that there are players who are naturally better-suited for point-per-reception leagues than others—guys like Wes Welker and Antonio Brown—but it also should change the way you construct your lineup in general.

On DraftKings, for example, you need to start someone in the flex spot. Wide receivers have a lot more merit as flex options in PPR leagues than standard scoring— perhaps even the preferred flex position. I think those guys who catch a lot of passes and, specifically, see a lot of targets are the ones who are also the most predictable from week to week. So those targets are something that I really pay for on a PPR site.

**Speaking of the flex, how do you handle it in tournaments? Do you always play a particular position?**

No, I don't always play one position. Basically, the main thing I want to do with the flex is use the player who is playing in the latest game (among the players that I like). So I select my players—whether it's three running backs or three receivers (with one in the flex)—and then I just use the player who has the latest possible game in the flex.

To give you an idea why I do that, I'll tell you about the DraftKings Millionaire Grand Final from 2013. Heading into the Monday night game, there were basically two players who could win the $1 million grand prize—me and a player named bundafever.

He was up by less than two points heading into the game and we each had one player left.

| RANK | TEAM NAME | PMR | FPTS |
|------|-----------|-----|------|
| 1 | Gateman07 (3) | 0 | 194.7 |
| 2 | bundafever | 60 | 193.14 |
| 3 | eritas2 | 0 | 192.1 |
| 4 | Al_Smizzle (3) | 60 | 191.44 |
| 5 | lilgordo (3) | 0 | 189.84 |
| 6 | TwoGun (8) | 0 | 188.24 |
| 7 | IllinSquad | 0 | 187.3 |
| 8 | mtolli11 (2) | 0 | 186.5 |
| 9 | maxdalury (30) | 0 | 186.1 |
| 10 | LaMagic (2) | 0 | 185.54 |

STANDINGS — find a rival... ✕ — GO TO MY TEAM(S) — ☐ Show Only Mine — Export Lineups to CSV

Bundafever's lone player was a running back. Looking at his guys who had already played and their salaries, I was able to reverse-engineer his lineup to figure out that he almost certainly had Frank Gore as his running back.

The problem was that I also had Gore, so the only way that I could catch him was to do a late swap to get Gore out of my lineup. Luckily, I placed Gore in the flex spot, so I was able to switch to Michael Crabtree. I still would have been able to do a late swap if I had Gore in my running back spot, but I would have needed to switch to a backup running back. Plus, by using Crabtree, I knew I'd have a unique lineup since bundafever had a running back, so I could potentially catch him. On the flip side, bundafever used Gore in the running back spot. If the standings were reversed and I had been ahead, he couldn't have swapped to Crabtree.

It didn't work out for me that time—I finished second and won $350,000—but the move gave me lots of different options.

The other thing that I like to do with the flex spot is use any player who might be listed as questionable. Obviously I'm not going to start someone if I think he'll be out, but sometimes guys are late scratches. If there's someone who I really like but he's questionable, I'll sometimes use him as the flex because, if he doesn't play, I'll have more options because I can sub to a bunch of different positions instead of just one.

## Do you ever pay up for kickers or defenses?

I'll pay for defenses that I like. Defenses can go a long way in determining tournament success, and they aren't as unpredictable as everyone thinks. Also, most people go with near-min-priced defenses, so paying a little more can help you field a unique lineup; it's a way to be contrarian without really using a sub-optimal strategy from a value standpoint.

As far as kickers, I rarely pay for those just because they're so volatile. I just search for the cheapest kicker who looks good—usually one in good weather or on a team with a good defense.

## Which traits/stats do you look for when selecting tournament lineups?

The main thing I look at is defensive vs. position stats. Those aren't as valuable in the beginning of the year (or else you need to use last year's stats), but they're more valuable by midseason or so. A lot of players look at the overall quality of a defense, but there are some good defenses that really struggle against one particular position, or bad defenses that can defend one position well. The Cardinals have had a decent defense recently but just can't stop the tight end, for example.

As far as finding particular players, one stat that I really like is 'percentage of supply.' Basically, I want to know what percentage of his team's targets a wide receiver or tight end eats up, or what percentage of carries a running back gets. I think that's a lot more valuable than most bulk stats. When a player receives a heavy workload and he's facing off against a defense that struggles against his position, that's usually a situation I want to target.

## CSURAM88's Analysis

The contrarian versus value topic is my favorite when it comes to tournaments. I think it's a really delicate issue that you need to balance because, all other things equal, you want the best values in your lineup. "All other things" aren't always equal, though, so going against the grain is smart at times.

I think it's still really more of an art than a science at this point. Part of that is because you don't really know what usage rates will look like prior to entering a tournament. You might have a decent idea of which players will be the most heavily utilized, but there are always surprises. Without knowing utilization exactly, you're left guessing, so that adds a little incentive to just go with the top values if you're unsure.

When it's very clear that a particular player or stack is going to be really heavily utilized, then I think it comes down to other factors, like the number of lineups you're submitting. If you have a bunch of entries into a tournament, you of course want some exposure to the "chalk," whereas players with just a single entry or two really need to consider a contrarian strategy a lot more seriously. If you have just a single shot to take down a tournament, you really want that lineup to be a unique one.

## Jonathan's Analysis

In *Fantasy Football (and Baseball) for Smart People*, I broke down the typical salary cap allocation for teams that win tournaments.

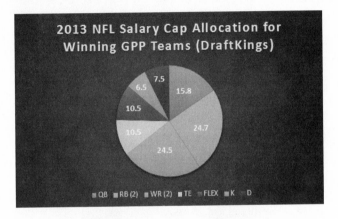

When you compare this with the typical salary cap allocation for winning 50/50 teams, there are two main differences. The first is that winning GPP lineups spend less at the quarterback position. Quarterback is by far the most consistent source of points in fantasy football; thus, it's smart to pay up for quarterbacks in cash games to ensure a high floor. That's not necessarily the case in tournaments, however; it can be extremely valuable to hit on an under-the-radar quarterback—yet more evidence that being a quality tournament player is about embracing volatility.

The second major difference is at defense, where winning GPP lineups are paying more, on average, than winning 50/50 lineups. Like Al_Smizzle mentioned, team defense isn't quite as unpredictable as some think, and paying up for one can also help you field a unique lineup. One of the best ways to gain an edge in tournaments is to hit on a defense that the rest of the field has overlooked.

As far as stacking a quarterback and wide receiver, the evidence is overwhelming that it increases upside.

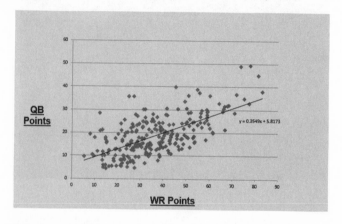

Only in rare circumstances should you not be stacking in NFL tournaments.

# Chapter 7: Lineup Creation with Naapstermaan

As much as projections and player values matter, they can be wasted if you can't construct a lineup in the proper manner. I spoke with naapstermaan about his lineup creation process for daily fantasy football.

Regarded as one of the game's top tournament players, naapstermaan has three GPP wins of at least $50,000, including a $125,000 win in DraftKings' 2013 MLB Midsummer Classic. In the same year, he won DraftKings' NBA Bankshot tournament.

| Rankings | naapstermaan |
| --- | --- |
| Overall updates weekly on Thursday. | |
| Overall Ranking | 46th (55301.26) |
| TPOY Ranking | 19th (11311.03) |
| Monthly Grinder Leaderboard | 34th (1214.49) |
| NFL Grinder Leaderboard | 63rd (5443.81) |
| MLB Grinder Leaderboard | 67th (7326.86) |
| NBA Grinder Leaderboard | 51st (17389.71) |

Naapstermaan is currently ranked in the top 20 for TPOY.

## What are the steps you take in creating a lineup?

Since I'm primarily a tournament player, I create more than one lineup each week. To get a sense of the pool of players I want to target for those lineups, I first start with the Vegas lines. That gives me an idea of who Vegas thinks will score the most points. I look not only at the total, but also the actual line to see which games are going to be close. I think that's one overlooked component of the lines; you always want players in games that are going to be close and high-scoring, if possible, because there's a synergistic effect there with the offenses feeding off one another.

The reason I like games to be close is because I want players who will have as many chances to score as possible; that's really what it's about in football—opportunities. I want running backs who will see a lot of touches, wide receivers who will get a lot of targets, and so on. I really weight those opportunity stats, especially in the red zone.

After I have an idea of who is going to score a lot of points and which players might benefit from that, I take a look at the site salaries. I look over the pricing just to get a general feel for it—who I think is naturally overpriced and underpriced, and how that matches up with what Vegas thinks. Sometimes you'll have a player who might do well but he just costs too much to play, or vice versa, a guy who is projected moderately but priced way too low.

I play on multiple sites, so I always shop around for the best prices. That's a really good way to get value without too much work. The site's salary algorithms are all different, so if one is really high on a player who the others aren't, that's probably a sign that he's overvalued on that single site. On the flip side, if he's cheap on just a single site, that's probably a good value opportunity.

Once you start playing more, you start to understand which sites value which stats. Some sites value recent stats more than others, for example, so knowing how sites value specific stats is important in understanding pricing and which players might be undervalued.

The last thing I do as the games are getting closer is check the weather, especially later in the year. That's an overlooked component of player projections and it's something Vegas can't capture in the initial lines because they have no idea what the weather is going to be like. Also, because so many users already have their lineups set before Sunday, they don't really have the weather factored in, so you can really use that to your advantage.

The weather really affects kickers the most. You really want to avoid kickers in windy games, especially. The same is true for quarterbacks.

I usually fill my lineups out on Sundays, so at that time, I basically combine all of the research and just toy around with different combinations of players until I find some that I like. There's a lot of give and take with trying to get those studs in there without going over the cap, so I'm looking to fit as many players that I really like into a single lineup as I can.

## How do you handle the flex on a full PPR site like DraftKings?

The flex is really interesting. It really depends on the pricing and the league. In general, I want guys who are going to get guaranteed touches in cash games. That's usually pass-catching running backs. They have high upside and they're also dependable.

In tournaments, I'll play whoever is the best value. A lot of times, I might start with a pass-catching running back and then swap to a wide receiver if I feel like that's best. There aren't as many quality running backs who are worth flex consideration, so it's easier to change from one of those to a receiver than vice versa. In general, though, I think those pass-catching running backs offer the best combination of upside and safety on DraftKings.

However, it's important not to get stuck on any single strategy. I don't always play one position or another in the flex; it really comes down to pricing and opportunities in a given week.

## How do you differentiate lineups for head-to-head or 50/50s vs. GPPs, if at all?

The biggest difference to me is that I want to play the best values in cash games, whereas in tournaments you really need to think outside of the box. That's especially true with the GPPs getting so big; there are so many people and so many different lineup combinations that users who can simultaneously both get value and have an outside-of-the-box lineup usually win.

In big GPPs, you're going to see different variations of basically every attractive player combination. If the Cowboys have a good matchup in a given week, you'll see all sorts of Romo-to-Dez lineups with a ton of different combinations around them, so it's really hard to gain an edge that way when you're going with the popular choices.

I think the best strategy for tournaments really comes down to how many lineups you're playing. I play a bunch, so I start covering different combos in the same way that I would in a cash game. I have enough lineups to still use a popular Romo-to-Dez pairing, for example. I still go against the grain, but if you have only a single lineup or two, you really need to think outside of the box with who you want to play.

It also comes down to risk tolerance. Going with players you know will be popular is probably your best bet to cash, but not the best way to win a tournament since there will be a lot of similarity in the field. Going with an outside-of-the-box lineup isn't the best way to cash, but it's often the most effective way to win.

One thing I like to do in tournaments is try to identify a situation or two that don't look good on paper but could end up better than expected. Maybe there's an injury no one is talking about, for example, that could really improve a particular player's projection for a game. If that's someone people are overlooking, I'll be more inclined to target that player.

### How much of your strategy in general is value-based versus being contrarian?

It's all value-based in cash games and a mix of value and being contrarian in tournaments. If you can hit on a player who isn't heavily owned in a GPP, that's huge and you'll have a really good chance to win it.

I don't bypass obvious values in tournaments, though. If there's a player who is really underpriced, I'm going to use him even if I think his usage will be really high; I won't fade a player just because of ownership percentages. So if a starting running back gets injured during the week and his backup is really cheap, that's a situation where I know other people will be on that player, but he's such a good value that I'm going to use him too. It's all about understanding how to best combine value and going against the grain. Plus, just because a player is a contrarian play doesn't mean he can't also be good value. The market isn't perfect so it's not like there's a black-and-white distinction between 'good value' and 'contrarian.'

Also, there are two different ways to look at 'value.' Usually, we talk about it in terms of a player's projection compared to his price. But 'value' in a tournament should also incorporate expected ownership. So let's say two wide receivers are both $5,000 on DraftKings and they're both projected at 13 points. Their value in a cash game would be the same, but in a tournament, the more valuable player is probably the one who will be the least popular. So there's just an additional component to deciphering value there in GPPs.

### How many different lineups do you play in a given day/week?

It just depends on the week. I play on multiple sites, so I naturally have more lineups. For novices, I'd suggest starting on one site and playing one lineup in cash games and then a few different lineups in GPPs. That will let you get comfortable figuring out how to win on a given site, how to manage your bankroll, and so on.

The number of total lineups and the overall amount of money that I play is the amount that, if I just have a horrible week and lose most or all of it, I won't feel terrible and won't be in a really bad spot with my bankroll. You never want to put yourself in a position where you'd be crippled if you tank in a given week.

In terms of the actual players, it again depends on the week. Sometimes there are a lot of players who I like, so I can diversify my lineups more, and sometimes there just aren't that many options. I never diversify so much that I'm just playing everyone and I never put a single player into every single one of my lineups, but the amount that I hedge depends on how many overall players I like and how much risk I want to take on that week.

My typical strategy revolves around finding one or two players I really like at each position, then building most of my lineups around different combinations of those players. Then, I use other players that I like as second-tier options just to act as a hedge. Overall, I usually play between five and 20 lineups in GPPs, depending on the week. If there's overlay, it's usually at the higher end of that range.

**Do you keep track of how you pair players in specific lineups so that you don't have too much exposure to certain groups of players?**

Yeah, I do. You can get in trouble if you're building lineups without any focus on how you're pairing players together, because that can really increase the risk you're taking on. If you like A.J. Green, Eddie Lacy, and Rob Gronkowski in a given week and you put 50 percent of the money you're playing on those players but you limit the number of times they're paired together, you'll be in a lot better spot than if you put 50 percent of your money on them but you put them all together in every lineup. If two of them have a bad game or something, you'll probably have an awful week no matter how the other players perform. Thinking of it in poker terms, you need to leave yourself 'outs.' You don't want to be in a position where you lose everything because of one or two fluke games.

I don't track the player exposure or player pairings in Excel or anything, but I'm always cognizant of it when I'm creating lineups. It's just a 'feel' thing; I might see I have too much of one player and I need to start working away from him, for example. I also build a general game plan before creating lineups, so I know I want around X amount of this player and Y amount of that player. If you just start blindly building lineups, you can get lost in it and take on a lot more risk than you're anticipating.

**Do you play a lot of Thursday-night leagues? Do you think they have an advantage over Sunday start times?**

I don't go crazy with Thursday-night leagues, but I think they have two advantages. One is that you can look at other teams to see what other people are thinking. So that can give you some extra information for your Sunday leagues.

The other advantage is that a lot of players want to force guys from the Thursday-night game into their lineups, so you can see some lower scores because the lineups aren't optimal. Don't underestimate how many users are playing just to watch their players on TV, especially in football.

Sometimes it makes sense to enter the Thursday-night leagues and then fade those players so you can get a lot less overlap with your lineup. Plus, there are a lot of stats showing that there isn't as much scoring in those games, so avoiding those players can be advantageous.

**How does league variance affect how you approach daily fantasy and how much money you play in a given week?**

I play a lot of tournaments, which have the highest variance, and you can run cold in those for a while just because they're so difficult to win. Knowing that, you can't put as much into them as you might put into your head-to-head or 50/50 action.

I think the best way to learn about variance and how much you should play is to just get in a bunch of different leagues. You'll start to get a sense of how often you'll win in each league type, what the payouts are like, and so on. You'll learn pretty quickly how much money is too much. There's really no better way to learn than a hands-on approach.

**Do you "pay" for certain positions or types of players? Do you ever pay to be contrarian at kicker or defense?**

For football, the one position that I typically pay for is tight end. There just aren't that many great tight end plays each week, so I prefer to go with one of the elite options when possible. I play Jimmy Graham a lot, for example, just because it's a source of points that people who aren't using him won't get. There's value in knowing that he's going to produce for you. So even if he isn't the best value in terms of his price tag, I like knowing that I'm going to get a certain floor of points when the other tight end options are crapshoots.

For kickers, I almost always go min-priced or near it in both cash games and tournaments. In cash games, I want sources of reliable points, and kickers just aren't reliable. They're too difficult to predict from week to week to justify paying for them. I think there's slightly more merit in doing it in tournaments just to be unique, but I still stay min-priced because of the unpredictability.

As far as defenses, I will spend more there because the matchup is so much more important. You have to get those defenses that are going to get pressure and are likely to force turnovers and even score touchdowns. Even though there's a lot of variance in football, it isn't like baseball where a stud hitter can go 0-for-5; the matchups matter more, so I'll pay up for an elite defense in a good matchup if I think they're going to score enough points to return value. And since most users still stick with low-priced Ds in GPPs, that's another advantage there.

## Do you always pair a quarterback with a wide receiver in tourneys? What about two or more of his wide receivers?

I usually stack a quarterback and wide receiver in tournaments. I start with just one receiver, and then I move to grouping QB-WR-WR on some of the more potent offenses. It just depends on the situation; I wouldn't do that on the Saints, for example, but I'll go QB-WR-WR on the Broncos all the time.

In general, though, the majority of my tournament lineups have a quarterback with one of his receivers. I like that because it's not normally likely that both wide receivers are going to have elite games, so I usually want the No. 1 option who will get the most targets, especially in the red zone. The lone exception is if the No. 1 is covered by an elite cornerback. In that case, I might take the No. 2 and pair him with his quarterback if I think he's going to see more targets than usual.

I'm actually not opposed to stacking in cash games in certain situations. I've even done QB-WR-WR in cash games when the top wide receiver was injured because the quarterback was elite and likely to spread the ball around, so there probably wasn't that much risk.

However, I don't always pair a quarterback and wide receiver; I think it's usually optimal, but it isn't something I do at all costs.

## Do you have any issue with playing a quarterback with his running back?

That's an interesting question and I've seen it win, but it's not something that I do. I think it can work, but I don't think it's optimal because you need a very specific game script to pan out; you need the offense to get up big early by passing, then the running back to have unusual success late in the game with a lead.

I think that if you're looking for two good games, a quarterback/running back duo could work. If you're looking for two great games, though, it probably isn't the best option. The only time I might try it is if 1) the running back can catch touchdowns and 2) the prices are relatively low. I wouldn't want to invest too much cap space in a pairing that is maybe a little bit fragile in terms of both guys generating elite production.

## Do you create lineups with projections? Is your process more subjective or stats-based?

It's more subjective for me. I think projections can work as a base for picking players, but you don't want to go solely off of projections because there's lot of different stuff that happens during a week—weather, injures—that changes the projections so much. It's good to have them to know who might be good value, but I personally still make subjective decisions on players as opposed to just letting an algorithm spit it out.

I also think that there's a whole lot that goes into creating quality lineups other than the projections, such as pairing players optimally or understanding what the rest of the field is going to do. What's optimal in a spreadsheet might not be optimal once you construct a lineup and enter leagues with other users trying to do the same thing as you. You have to think not only about the projections, but also about how you can get the biggest possible advantage on the field.

In terms of stats, I obviously still use them, and I look primarily at projected workload (attempts, targets, carries) and matchup stuff (defense vs. position). I actually use stats a lot, and I use them to help me make better subjective decisions. So I guess you'd say I'm subjective, but informed by objective research. It's a combination, really.

**As a tournament specialist, anything else you'd like to add about GPP play?**

My biggest piece of advice is to continue to test out different strategies and really think about how you can be unique. With daily fantasy growing so much, the tournaments are so big that basically every possible strategy is covered in these leagues. Players are learning so much and everyone is getting better at finding the optimal plays that it really benefits you to go against the grain and really consider how you can gain an advantage with a strategy that people are missing. In short, it can be less about value and more about just figuring out how you can get the biggest edge.

## CSURAM88's Analysis

One of the really interesting topics here is tracking player exposure. I think this is really, really important, and something that I'm always trying to improve. One new technique I'm using is providing each player with a grade for both cash games in tournaments. I'll use my model and projections to figure out his upside/floor, then determine how much value he could have to me in different league types. Then I'll use those grades to determine player exposure, with higher-graded players obviously making their way into more of my lineups.

It's also important to keep track of the way you pair players. You can really significantly increase the amount of risk you're assuming without even knowing it if you have a certain group of players always together in lineups. You might think you're diversifying when you're actually taking on a high level of risk, so understanding exposure to both individual players and player combinations is vital. It's also something that's really easy to track, even if you just write it down, but a lot of players overlook it.

## Jonathan's Analysis

Naapstermaan touched on some aspects of daily fantasy leagues that start on Thursday nights, and I've done a bunch of research on both Thursday-night leagues and the Thursday NFL games in general.

First, take a look at the average scores in DraftKings Thursday and Sunday GPPs.

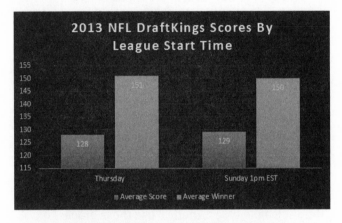

In theory, winning GPP scores should be higher in Thursday night leagues because there's one extra game from which to choose, and thus a larger pool of potential players. The more players, the higher the winning score should be, and that's exactly what we see in reality.

However, the average score overall is lower in Thursday night leagues than in those that start on Sunday. That suggests that, although the top daily fantasy players are approaching Thursday night leagues optimally, the crowd isn't; they're likely forcing players from the

Thursday game into their lineups just so they can watch them play.

Ultimately, I'd say your chances of winning a Thursday-night league are the same as any other, or maybe slightly better, but your odds of cashing are higher because of an abundance of "dead" lineups.

In terms of Thursday-night production, here's a look at how teams have performed in Thursday night games.

### Passing Yards

There's a shocker right off of the bat. In every season since 2009, teams have combined for more passing yards in Thursday night games than all other games.

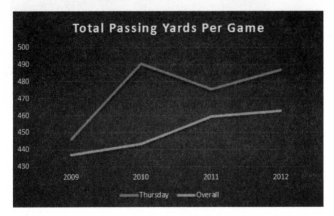

The numbers are actually pretty drastic, too. In 2010, for example, the offenses playing in the 10 Thursday night games combined for 490.6 passing yards per game—nearly 50 more yards than the overall mark.

### Passing Touchdowns

However, the passing success hasn't translated into scores. There have been more passing touchdowns per game overall than in the Thursday night games alone in all four seasons studied.

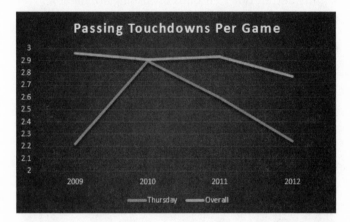

Again, these results are pretty clear. So why in the world are teams racking up yards through the air, but they can't pass the ball into the end zone?

I don't think this is a sample size issue because, over the past four years, there have been 46 Thursday night games. That's enough to suggest the big gaps in passing touchdowns actually mean something.

Before forming any sort of hypothesis, let's examine the rushing numbers.

### Rushing Yards

While teams have lit it up through the air in Thursday night matchups, they've struggled accumulating yards on the ground.

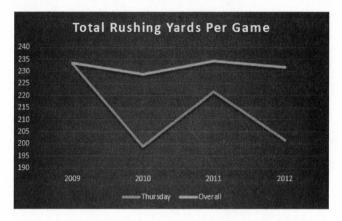

Over the past three seasons, especially, offenses just haven't had much Thursday night rushing success.

### Rushing Touchdowns

Finally, note that teams have rushed for fewer touchdowns on Thursday night in three of four seasons.

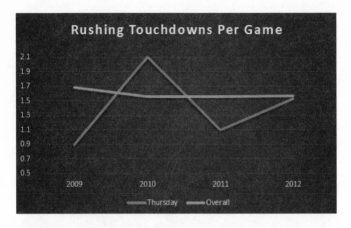

There's a small effect here, but probably not enough to be meaningful. While it makes sense that offenses would score less in Thursday games, and thus rush for fewer touchdowns, we really can't conclude anything from this data.

So what the heck are we supposed to make of these numbers? Here's my answer: I have no freakin' clue. The only possible answer that I have is that, since the NFL knows people are going to tune into Thursday night games no matter what, they don't seem to care much about the quality of the matchup.

Frequently, it seems as though 1) the Thursday night teams are below-average as a whole and 2) the games aren't very close. That could lead to more passing from the losing team that's not completely balanced out by more running from the winning team, inflating the total passing yardage. But since the teams are often slightly worse than in your typical matchup, there's less scoring overall.

Or I could be completely wrong.

Still, there appears to be some actionable data here. Even if we don't know *why* offenses generally seem worse on Thursday night except when it comes to racking up passing yards, it's still useful to know that a short week, for whatever reason, doesn't appear to affect the passing game as much as the running game.

## Chapter 8: Building a Bankroll with KillaB2482

I was introduced to KillaB2482 through the guys at RotoGrinders, and I instantly recognized that he's a very shrewd mind in daily fantasy sports. The interesting thing about KillaB2482 is that he's a very specialized player, concentrating almost exclusively on the NFL.

| Rankings | KillaB2482 |
|---|---|
| Overall updates weekly on Thursday. | |
| Overall Ranking | 11th (158477.19) |
| TPOY Ranking | 2838th (179.31) |
| NFL Grinder Leaderboard | 2nd (158170.83) |
| NBA Grinder Leaderboard | 3835th (136.00) |

With most top daily fantasy players going hard in multiple sports, it's amazing that KillaB2482 is currently the 11th-ranked player in the world despite playing only one sport significantly. Within football, though, he's the No. 2-ranked player, playing a huge amount of volume and seeing all kinds of success.

KillaB2482 is a former poker pro—he graduated with an Economics degree in 2005 and quit his job as a consumer lender to play poker full-time—and he has shown sustained success in daily fantasy sports. His biggest week of daily fantasy football involved over $100,000 in profit. Given his poker background and how much emphasis he places on treating daily fantasy as an investment, KillaB2482 is the perfect player to give advice on bankroll management.

## Talk about your general bankroll management philosophy.

I really believe that bankroll management is the most crucial skill in all of daily fantasy sports. If you can't properly manage a bankroll, you're going to go broke, regardless of how much you win. You need to adhere to strict bankroll guidelines to be a profitable player. The goal is to maximize profits, too; you want to make as much money as possible without taking on too much risk to the point that you could go bankrupt.

Personally, I don't play more than 15 percent of my bankroll on any single lineup, and that's if I'm using it conservatively in heads-up leagues, for example. I might play more than 15 percent if I'm using more than one lineup or collection of core players.

The key is understanding how much to play with multiple lineups is knowing how much overlap you have. If you change just a single player, that's basically the same lineup and you probably shouldn't play more than 15 percent. If you have two totally separate lineups, you might be able to play, say, 20 percent of your bankroll in cash games—15 percent on the top lineup and five percent on the second lineup. You could also play 10 percent on each (or whatever combination you'd like) if you think the lineups are equal in expected value.

That second lineup would act almost as a hedge against the top lineup tanking. So while it might be optimal in a vacuum to play just a single lineup, it could actually be optimal to the safety of your bankroll to use one as a small hedge. Plus, you're still playing a near-optimal lineup as that No. 2 option; it's not like you're just picking anyone.

But again, I think the main idea is that the more differentiation there is between two lineups, the more you can play. If you have two mutually-exclusive lineups, I'd advise playing as much (but no more) than 20 percent of your bankroll in cash games. The more overlap, the more variance, and the less you can play without taking on a lot of risk.

Also, keep in mind that you don't want to spread yourself too thin. Playing three or four lineups in cash games might be safe in that you won't lose a lot of money at once, but you're also unlikely to be profitable since you'll need to choose so many players. In that case, you'd likely slowly lose money. It's just a balance between using optimal players, maximizing profitability, and limiting risk.

A final downside of using too many lineups—one that's overlooked quite a bit—is managing them just before kickoff. If you have a couple last-minute scratches, it can become somewhat difficult to properly manage multiple lineups. Even if you get the injured players out, the lineups might no longer be +EV if you have to force sub-optimal players in there.

### How do you allocate your money in play to various league types? What percentage is in GPPs, head-to-heads, and so on?

Well, I usually stick to one cash game lineup on each site where I play. I like the variance of that, and I think it's ideal for me personally over the long run. When I talk about cash games, I mean any league where more than 30 percent of users are paid. That would include head-to-head games, 50/50s, and three-man leagues. All of those are low-variance games in which you can play a higher percentage of your bankroll. In those cash games, like I said, I'll put no more than 15 percent on my optimal lineup.

In GPPs, I'll play multiple lineups using primarily high-ceiling players. The amount of money you place into tournaments really depends on each player. Some people don't want to grind out profits and are just playing daily fantasy to hit a home run. They might deposit $1,000 and use it all to take chances winning a large-field GPP. So they might play $100 for 10 straight weeks, solely in tournaments.

In terms of being long-term profitable and grinding out profits while remaining +EV, though, I wouldn't put a huge amount of my bankroll into tournaments—around one part to every five parts in cash games, or somewhere around three percent. GPPs are high-variance and you can go on cold streaks. At three percent, you're looking at no more than $30 per week for a $1,000 bankroll.

The cash games are going to be the constant stream of income for most players. In GPPs, you really need to finish in the top couple percent to really see a return, so most of the time, even for good players, you're going to lose money.

You can of course roll out multiple GPP lineups to reduce some of the variance. I personally use a few different tournament lineups that I like—high-upside lineups—but I'm still not playing more than three or four percent of my total bankroll on those lineups (in total, not individually).

## What are the biggest bankroll management misconceptions?

I have a poker background, and in poker, a lot of inexperienced players think there's just one right way to play a hand. Similarly, I think the biggest bankroll misconception in daily fantasy is that there's one magic formula that's ideal and going to lead to profits no matter what. There's not just one way to profit in daily fantasy sports; some pros play only cash games or only tournaments, for example.

There are certain principles that you should understand—like not placing 50 percent of your bankroll into a single tournament lineup, for example—but there are different ways to reach the same result. The specific path that's best for you really depends on your lineups, risk tolerance, league selection, and so on.

Just consider typical payouts in different leagues. If you play someone of the same skill level as you in a 50/50, you'll win once every two days, on average. If you play a 1,000-man GPP with the top 200 paid out, however, you'll win once every five days. Just from those numbers alone you can see that there necessarily must be different bankroll management paths.

**How does bankroll management change, if at all, for NFL since the games are just once a week? Do you play a higher percentage than in other sports?**

It shouldn't change too much just because the games are only once a week. You can't just start spending half of your bankroll each week because you need more action. That's a big mistake I see people make. They play MLB where they can play every day, and then NFL rolls around and they feel like they aren't playing enough because they're reinvesting only 15 or 20 percent each week.

The one thing that comes with NFL play that's unique is that, because there's so much action, you can be a little pickier with your league selection. There are so many players that it's a lot easier to be the favorite in a head-to-head match, for example. So if you find that you're really a much more profitable player in NFL than other sports because of the weaker competition, then that's a situation where you might change your bankroll management just a little.

Eventually, there's going to be a lot of weaker opponents in every sport as the daily fantasy industry grows, but there's already a great money-making opportunity in NFL with all of the players migrating over from season-long leagues.

## At what point do you think someone can know if their profitability is the result of truly being a long-term winner?

It's very tough to reach "the long run" in football because the season is so short. There are only 17 days to play leagues in football, at least during the regular season, compared to hundreds in baseball. Each MLB season is the equivalent of playing over 10 seasons of NFL, so daily fantasy baseball players can know if they're profitable a whole lot faster than daily fantasy football players.

That results in two things. First, there are some bad players who could end up being profitable during a season of NFL even though they aren't long-term winners. That can be bad if they start to play as though they're long-term profitable when they aren't. You also see players who are actually very skilled who might go an entire season without winning in football. There's just a lot of variance, so it's important to know how difficult it is to reach the long run.

One trick you can do to reach the long run quicker is to play more lineups, even if they aren't completely optimal. So maybe you think your top lineup can win 65 percent of head-to-head games and your second lineup can win 60 percent. You'll still be profitable playing both lineups because you can take more chances (play more money) with two lineups, assuming they don't overlap too much. You don't want to play just to play because you can slowly lose money, but it can be smart to play two lineups if you think they're both going to be profitable.

An example of this might be playing $1,000 on one lineup that will win 65 percent of the time versus $800 on one that will win at that same rate and $400 on one that will win 60 percent of the time. You could just play $1,200 on the optimal lineup, but that would be riskier and take you longer to reach the long run. The profits might not be quite as good playing a second lineup that's not quite as optimal, but as long as it will still be profitable, it limits risk so you can guarantee reaching long-term profitability.

It's basically a version of "Would you rather have $1 million or a 50 percent chance at $2.2 million?" In terms of expected value, the second option is clearly better, but most people would take the $1 million because it's a sure thing.

Basically, the more lineups you play, the more data you'll have on if you are profitable. But again, you don't want to spread yourself too thin, so it's a balance. But to give you an idea of how much variance there can be in football, my return has been as high as 70 percent in a single season, but also as low as five percent. The latter is close to not even being profitable over the course of 17 weeks.

## Does the amount you play change based on your confidence in a lineup?

It foes, but it's a small factor. It's not as much my confidence in my lineup as it is in the individual players who I like, but I might play just a little more if I really feel like I have an advantage. One of the problems is that it's difficult to predict how well a lineup is really going to do, so you can't have too much more confidence in Lineup Y than Lineup X. Normally, I'm around that 15-percent mark for cash games.

One aspect of football that changes my confidence in players or lineups is injuries. There are so many injuries by midseason that we really see changes in production. If you can accurately predict how those injuries will change a team's output, that's a big advantage—more of an edge than I think you can have to start the year when everyone is healthy.

**What are your thoughts on assessing risk as a function of player exposure, i.e. more about the amount of money on each player and player combinations than the lineup?**

Yeah, daily fantasy is exactly like the stock market in that way. Each player is a stock, and you have to 1) figure out how much you want to invest in each stock and 2) determine how to configure those stocks to maximize your return.

Personally, I rarely have 100 percent of my money on a single player. I have to really, really like a player to put him in every cash game lineup. Normally, the most I'll put into any single player is 60 to 70 percent. It just depends on how much I like a player and how many other options there are at his position.

I definitely analyze players individually, though, as opposed to looking at how much money is on each lineup. Again, the amount of money you can place on two different lineups depends on the overlap. That's why it's important to determine the confidence you have in each player and how much of the money you're playing that week can realistically be invested in him.

**How do you know when to take some shots? Are there ever situations when you deem it appropriate to be more aggressive with your bankroll?**

You should take more shots when the odds are in your favor. The most obvious time that this happens is when there's overlay. When there's big overlay, nearly everyone in the tournament can have a positive expected return because the site is losing money on the league. There was some huge overlay to start the season on DraftKings last year, for example, and it made sense to get more action that day.

Basically, there's a positive correlation between overlay and the pool of acceptable players; the more overlay, the more players you can start without being –EV. So when there's "extra" money in a prize pool due to overlay, that's when I'll take more chances.

Another aspect of tournament play that changes how aggressive I am is the percentage of entrants who get paid. That's one big positive with DraftKings since they pay at least 20 percent of users in most GPPs. That allows you to be a lot more aggressive in how you approach them.

This relates back to overlay, too. If there's a 1,000-man GPP that pays out the top 200 users, but it fills with only 800 people, there's now not only free money in the league, but you also need to finish only in the top 25 percent of users to cash instead of the top 20 percent.

You're not only +EV, but you can also expect to cash at a higher rate.

You have to be careful to still stick within your bankroll guidelines, though. When there's a lot of overlay and I want to get in more GPPs, for example, I'll typically hold off on some cash game action to balance things out. I'm still taking on more risk, but it's warranted given that the profitability will be greater in the tournaments with overlay.

The other way to balance out some of the risk with playing more tournament lineups is simply to diversify the player pool to a greater degree. That means making more lineups and selecting a wider range of players. That way, you'll have some built-in safety while taking the risk of placing more money in GPPs. Some weeks, I'll play as many as 30 GPP lineups if there's a lot of overlay. When there's not, I might play just five tournament lineups per week.

Still, you can't just place 50 percent of your bankroll into a tournament because there's overlay; it's no guarantee of cashing. Outside of overlay situations, I pretty much have the same approach each week from a bankroll management perspective.

## Do you treat qualifiers the same as regular GPPs from a bankroll management standpoint?

I put qualifiers in the same category as normal GPPs in terms of my lineup, but in a different category in terms of bankroll management. The reason is that short-term profits for qualifiers are scarcer than in other GPPs since you often win a ticket into another tournament. That means the chances of seeing actual cash are basically the probability of winning a ticket multiplied by the chances of cashing in the next tournament.

If you have a 25 percent chance of winning a ticket and a 20 percent chance of cashing in the next tournament with that ticket, for example, you'll end up cashing on only five percent of such qualifiers that you enter—1-in-20. That's important to know and obviously changes how you need to approach things from a bankroll standpoint.

## What are your thoughts on getting investors as a daily fantasy player?

Yeah, I've personally used investors in the past and it's a great way to play more money without taking on more financial risk. If you can show people you've been profitable in the past, you could potentially sell part of yourself as a daily fantasy player for X dollars.

So maybe you have a $1,000 bankroll and you want to grow that to $5,000. You could charge $100 for every one percent of your future profits. So to get to $5,000, you'd need to give away 40 percent of your future profits.

The downside is that you could limit your future upside, especially if you think you're a true long-term profitable player, but you can also expedite the process of bankroll growth without taking huge risks that could leave you bankrupt, so it's something to consider.

## CSURAM88's Analysis

One topic that's interesting when it comes to bankroll management is how player and lineup diversification affects the amount you can play. I think that's really important when assessing your potential profitability.

Some players do everything they can to maximize their win percentage, which is good, but sometimes you can do things that maybe aren't as optimal while also increasing profitability. That's the idea behind hedging; if your No. 2 or No.3 lineups are still +EV, then you definitely want to play them. Not only do you have more money in play and greater potential profits, but you also have more safety; with a greater pool of players comes less risk.

It all comes down to balancing the player pool with optimizing your return. It's not just a question of your ROI, though; you also need to assess risk, and opening up the player pool a little bit can limit some of your downside. There's value in just staying in the game so that, if you do have an edge, you can eventually see it.

In terms of playing greater volume based on confidence, the only time I do that is if there's late news that gives me a really big advantage over the field. So if I know that Matthew Stafford is going to be really heavily utilized and he's surprisingly ruled out five minutes before kickoff, I'll definitely take more action because I know I'm going to have an advantage over the field with a lot of users keeping him in their lineups.

It's the same idea as getting in more leagues because of overlay; if I have a really good reason to think that my expected win percentage is higher than normal, I'll play more. It needs to extend beyond me just liking the players in my lineup, though, because I don't think the amount you like your lineup in a vacuum is really going to help predict how successful it will be. Basically, it has to be when I have good reason to believe that the herd is going to make a collective mistake.

## Jonathan's Analysis

One of the things that initially attracted me to DraftKings is the tournament payout structure; most GPPs pay out at least 20 percent of entrants, which dramatically changes the risk inherent to each league. When you can expect to cash in one out of every five leagues, you can approach a tournament much differently than if it's one out of 10.

As KillaB mentioned, one of the outcomes of a flatter payout structure is that you probably don't need to diversify your lineups quite as much in order to minimize risk. If you play five totally different lineups in a league that pays out 20 percent of entrants, for example, you have a 50 percent chance of cashing in a given week. Those are decent odds when you're simultaneously increasing your upside in a major way.

As mentioned, the exception is qualifiers in which you aren't paid out in cash, but rather in tickets. The "end game" in qualifiers comes not after the qualifier, but after the resulting tournament. That significantly alters the risk involved in qualifiers such that you can't approach them in the same way as normal GPPs. Note that this doesn't make qualifiers a poor investment—they can allow you to get into big tournaments at a cheap price, and they also often have overlay—but be careful with them.

One of the other aspects of bankroll management to which I subscribe is analyzing risk as a function of player exposure, not in regards to actual lineups. The following is a lessons I wrote in GrindersU over at RotoGrinders.

> *"How many lineups do you play each day?" We see that question tossed around quite a bit in the RotoGrinders forums, don't we? It's a worthwhile inquiry, but sometimes we get a little too obsessed over lineups, forgetting that the most important thing is selecting player combinations in a manner that limits risk and/or promotes upside as much as possible.*

## Player Exposure

*Let's say you're playing on a site that requires two pitchers and eight hitters and you want to play two different lineups. How many different players are you going to use? Well, you could use as many as 20 players, but you could also roster as few as 11.*

*In the latter scenario, your two lineups would have the same group of core players—nine players the same—with just a single player different in each. In terms of risk/reward, such a lineup combination is dramatically different from playing two completely different lineups.*

*The former lineup combination—two with just a single player (or two) different—isn't much different from playing just one "optimal" lineup. It's a smart move if you're undecided between two players or just want to diversify a bit while maintaining upside. Meanwhile, two completely different lineups—or two lineups with just a couple players the same—is a high-floor/low-ceiling play. You're less likely to see a rapid bankroll decline, but you're also unlikely to witness quick growth.*

*The point here is that what we should be worried about isn't the number of lineups, but the total exposure to each player.*

Analyzing player exposure in terms of the diversity of your lineups is a more accurate way to assess risk than just counting lineups.

## Postface

So that's it. If you enjoyed *Daily Fantasy Pros Reveal Their Money-Making Secrets*, check out the rest of the *Fantasy Football for Smart People* book series on Amazon or FantasyFootballDrafting.com. At the latter site, I also sell my Weekly In-Season Package, draft packages, and individual issues of RotoAcademy—my fantasy football training school.

Speaking of RotoAcademy, the best value is to enroll. You'll get book-length PDFs with written and video content every month, delivered right to your email. Whatever rate you get will be locked in forever (so you'll keep paying the same amount even after the "tuition" increases for new students in the future).

Don't forget that I'm giving away some freebies, too. The first is 10 percent off anything you purchase on my site—all books, all rankings, all draft packages, and even past issues of RotoAcademy. Just go to FantasyFootballDrafting.com and use the code "Smart10" at checkout to get the savings.

By JONATHAN BALES

Visit FantasyFootballDrafting.com and
enter 'Smart10' at checkout to get 10% off your purchase.

The second freebie is an entire issue of RotoAcademy.
Go to FantasyFootballDrafting.com for your free issue
(RotoAcademy Issue II), add the item to your cart, and
enter "RA100" at checkout to get it free of charge.

And lastly, I've partnered with DraftKings to give you a
100 percent deposit bonus when you sign up there to
play daily fantasy football. Deposit through
DraftKings.com/Bales to get the bonus, use the
"Smart10" code to buy my in-season package at
FantasyFootballDrafting.com (complete with DraftKings
values all year long), and start cashing in on your hobby.

Again, one reader who purchased my in-season package
last year has won $25,000 in multiple daily fantasy
leagues.

Thanks so much for your continued interest in the *Fantasy Football for Smart People* series. It's been a joy to write this stuff, especially if it helps you win a league or two this year.

GET SOME!

## Bonus Material

The following is an excerpt from my book *Fantasy Football (and Baseball) for Smart People: How to Turn Your Hobby into a Fortune*. This chapter contains information on conquering cash games. The book, which you can buy on Amazon, makes for an excellent complement to this one with highly actionable data on what's really winning daily fantasy leagues.

## One-on-One: How to Win Heads-Up Leagues (and 50/50s)

*"Success is steady progress toward one's personal goals."*

- *Jim Rohn*

You know what I like to discuss with my friends who play daily fantasy? Tournaments. GPPs. Large-field leagues. Whatever you want to call it, we like to talk about how awesome it would be to win one million bucks on DraftKings.

You know what most pros like to discuss? Head-to-heads and 50/50s. Many of daily fantasy's top players build their bankroll by kicking ass in cash games. They take advantage of tournaments, too, but they utilize smaller leagues for steadier growth.

Head-to-heads and other small leagues that pay out a high percentage of entrants are foundational pieces of the daily fantasy pie. The upside isn't as great as in a tournament, but neither is the risk. And if you're really trying to see a quality ROI in daily fantasy, you need to minimize risk in some form or another.

There are two primary ways in which head-to-head leagues in particular minimize risk. First, the obvious: there are only two freakin' players. Even if you're new to daily fantasy, you'll still probably win at least 40 percent of your heads-up matches.

Second, head-to-head leagues allow for a linear return. By that, I mean that if you consistently finish in the top 25 percent of all scores, you'll get paid at that rate (winning in three-quarters of your heads-up leagues). If you're a totally average player near the 50th percentile, you'll probably win right around as many as you lose.

That's in opposition to tournaments in which you need to cross a certain tipping point to get paid. A 50th percentile score isn't going to do you any good; it will never win.

## 50/50s

Like a heads-up league, the top half of entrants in a 50/50 get paid. That can create safety if you're entering just one lineup. No matter the quality of your lineup in a heads-up match, there's always a chance that it gets beat by a higher score. That won't happen in a 50/50, however, since you won't see an outlier take you down.

However, here's why head-to-head games are safer when we look at the broad picture: the more you play, the less risky they become. With head-to-heads, you can enter the same lineup again and again and actually *increase* the safety of that lineup; the larger the sample size, the more likely that you'll get paid "as you should," i.e. there will be a linear relationship between your score and your return.

If you have a top 10 percent score, for example, and enter it into just one league, you'll have a 90 percent chance to win. Enter it into 10 leagues, and the odds of not getting paid are basically zero. Enter it into 1,000 leagues, and you'll be nearly guaranteed to win close to 90 percent and lose close to 10 percent.

Now consider a single lineup in 50/50s. One 50/50? Lots of safety. Two 50/50s. A little less safety. Five-hundred 50/50s? You better be on your game, bro. Because if that team flops and you entered it into nothing but 50/50s, you just lost all of your money.

Heads-up leagues are like schools of fish: they have safety in numbers. Meanwhile, 50/50s are similar to pancakes. As Mitch Hedberg would have said, they're all exciting at first, but after a while you're fucking sick of 'em.

## Diversifying Based on Player Pool

Theoretically, 50/50s would be invaluable if you were playing completely different lineups. You could enter various lineups into different 50/50s and just use those to grow your bankroll.

The problem with that strategy is that, as you move down your list of lineups, they become less and less optimized. The value of submitting one lineup into lots of leagues is that you can play the best of the best. Over the long-run, that will provide you with the best return.

So it's really a balancing act between diversifying lineups and increasing upside. That means your potential player pool—the number of players you like in a given night in MLB or a given weekend in the NFL—should dictate your strategy.

Namely, if you like relatively few players, you'll have fewer lineups and would be smart to play in more head-to-head matchups. Meanwhile, a larger player pool would allow for greater lineup diversity, and thus more opportunity to enter 50/50s.

## Raise the ~~Roof~~ Floor

One of the most overrated stats in all of football is yards-per-carry (YPC). The stat is pretty much useless because it's so affected by outliers. A running back can be having a poor game of 15 carries for 45 yards (3.0 YPC), then break off a 70-yard run that will catapult his average to 7.19 YPC. All of a sudden, he "ran all over the defense"—a conclusion that might result from one broken tackle or a defender falling down.

Is that 115 yards on 16 carries really the same as a running back who continually gashes the defense for seven yards? Of course not, and it's vital to understand that difference when selecting your fantasy lineups.

In his book Antifragile, Nassim Nicholas Taleb makes a distinction between the robust and the antifragile. The robust can withstand shock; it remains the same in the face of outliers. The antifragile, on the other hand, not only withstands variance, but it prospers from it. The antifragile *improves* with chaos.

In many ways, your daily fantasy lineup selection should be built upon a similar foundation. Outlying poor performances will hurt you regardless of the league type, obviously, but you want your head-to-head lineups to be as resilient as possible; you want consistent play from every position. When a 40th percentile lineup is a winner in 50/50s and most head-to-heads, you want low-variance, not volatility.

## Understanding Long-Term Trends

In any daily fantasy sport, you have a lot of decisions on your hands, the most overlooked of which might be salary cap allocation. The individual matchups are of course important and every lineup should be built upon specific information relative to that day's games, but I think some players overlook the importance of long-term trends.

While the value of an individual player is fleeting, the importance and consistency of specific positions is more everlasting. Are quarterbacks generally safer options than running backs? Is it ever okay to pay up for a kicker? Which types of wide receivers provide consistent production?

## NFL Head-to-Head and 50/50 Strategy

Head-to-head or 50/50, what you're seeking is consistency. If you average 150 points with half of your lineups scoring 100 points and the other half scoring 200 points, you're actually not going to be a profitable heads-up player. If you can find a way to score around 150 points each time, however, you'll be nearly unbeatable over the long-run.

To back up that idea, let's take a look at some more DraftKings data, this time on the average scores in different league types. Of all the charts you'll see in this book, this one will probably end up being the most popular because of all the information it contains.

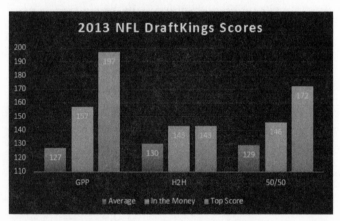

This is awesome stuff. I'm going to get into more detail on the GPP section in the next chapter, but you can see the average top score (197) and average score that finishes in the money (157) dwarf the numbers in head-to-heads and 50/50s.

Looking at those head-to-head and 50/50 leagues, the average top score in the latter is much higher than that in the former, which is to be expected since there are just more lineups (sometimes many more so) in 50/50s. Nothing strange there.

But here's what's most interesting to me. The average "in the money" score in head-to-heads (143) is three points lower than that in 50/50s (146). Since the top half of entrants get paid in both league types and we're dealing with a huge sample size, you'd expect the numbers to be equal. You'll have more outliers in a 50/50 since there are more lineups, but if you took the same sample of heads-up lineups, you'd think that the score distribution and average would be the same.

But it's not. Further, despite a higher average "in the money" score in 50/50s, the average overall score is one point *lower* than in head-to-head leagues. That means the deviation between the average score and the average winning score in 50/50s (17 points) is a lot higher than the same deviation in heads-up matches (only 13 points).

Here's my explanation for the difference that, if true, could really alter the way you enter both league types: *people are approaching 50/50 leagues with the wrong strategy*. It initially seems like 50/50s might be more difficult since the average "in the money" score is three points higher than in heads-up matches, but I don't think that's the case.

Instead, I think many daily fantasy players are approaching 50/50s with a high-variance strategy much like what you might seek in a GPP. So there's a wide gap between the best scores and the average scores that increases the overall average, but *the outlying top lineups might be throwing off the mean*.

Here's a visualization. First, this is how scores might be distributed in a 10-man 50/50 league in which players submit optimal lineups.

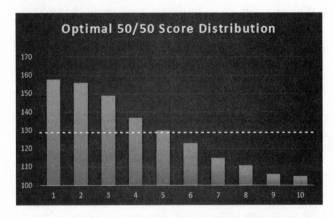

This sample distribution matches the DraftKings data—an average "in the money" score of 146 and an average overall score of 129. The dotted line represents that average. You can see that half of the 10 lineups finish above that 129 mean, which is what we'd expect if players submit lineups as they should with a low-variance strategy in mind.

However, this is an example of what we actually see with 50/50 lineups.

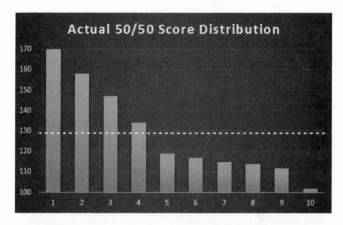

Again, the average of the "in the money" scores is still 146 and the overall mean is still 129. But there's a larger deviation in scores, so the top lineups make it seem as though players are better when they're really just submitting high-risk/high-reward lineups.

Now, here's the important part. Take a look at the average lineup dotted line. It's still at 129, but now there are only four lineups that fall above it. The fifth-best lineup—one that would cash in this 50/50 league—has just 119 points, which is 10 below the overall average.

So despite the higher average score in 50/50s over head-to-heads, the deviation in points suggests *you might be able to cash in them more easily*. Daily fantasy players might see the large number of entrants in a 50/50 (which can be huge at times) and automatically think they need a high-variance lineup with lots of upside. That creates a phenomenon through which below-average lineups can sneak into the money.

In reality, you should approach a 50/50 just like a head-to-head league. In both, you want a high floor.

## NFL Position Consistency

For the most part, daily fantasy players don't pay much for kickers. Amateurs and pros alike understand that it's usually senseless to pay top-dollar for a position that's not consistent from week to week. It doesn't matter how many points a player scores and it doesn't matter how scarce those points are if you can't predict his performance.

We all seem to intuitively know that we shouldn't pay for kickers, but few people extend this argument to the other positions. In leagues in which safety is the name of the game, there should be a strong positive correlation between the percentage of cap space you're willing to spend on a player and your ability to accurately project his performance.

It's not like any of the skill positions are unpredictable in the same way as kickers, but there's still varying degrees of predictability. Those should undoubtedly have an influence on your decision-making. All other things equal, you could maximize your team's long-term floor by allocating a higher percentage of the cap to the safest players.

In my first book on daily fantasy, I calculated the consistency of each position. I'm going to use the same methodology here, but with updated results. To obtain the numbers, I looked at the top fantasy scorers over the past four years. They are the players who would typically cost the most money on daily fantasy sites.

I charted the number of "startable" weeks for the players at each position. A "startable" week was defined as finishing in the top 33 percent at the position (among the top 30 quarterbacks, tight ends, defenses, and kickers and the top 75 running backs and wide receivers).

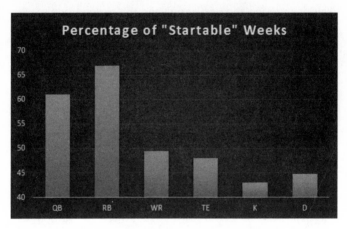

You can see that running backs have been by far the most consistent position, with the best of the bunch giving you a top 10 performance 67.0 percent of the time. Quarterbacks aren't far behind at 61.1 percent, but no other position is close.

When you think about it, that shouldn't be a surprise. Consider the number of opportunities each position has per game. For quarterbacks, it might be 35 attempts. For top running backs, it's in the range of 15 to 25 touches.

Meanwhile, wide receivers and tight ends might be lucky to see 10 targets in a game, and it's often much fewer. Just based on those numbers alone, you'd expect quarterbacks and running backs to be more consistent, and thus more predictable. It's like asking if a baseball player will come closer to hitting at his career average after five games or after 20 games. . .there's just no contest.

Taking it a step further, I analyzed the percentage of "top-tier" weeks turned in by each position. I defined "top-tier" as a top two finish for quarterbacks, tight ends, kickers, and defenses or a top five finish for running backs and wide receivers (the top 6.7 percent for each position).

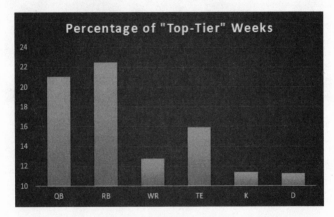

Again, no contest. Quarterbacks and running backs are just far more consistent on a week-to-week basis than all other positions. When you're paying for reliability, you should start with the quarterback and running back positions.

## NFL Player Types

The position consistency data is certainly useful in all league types, but we can cut up the data a little more to obtain even better accuracy. Specifically, we can look at subsections of each position to see which *types* of players are the most consistent, and thus worthy of the majority of our cap space in head-to-head leagues.

Before diving into that, I think it's important to once again rehash the fact that much of what we view as individual consistency and volatility in the NFL is illusory. Would we ever create enduring narratives for baseball players through eight games? Never, so why do it for NFL players?

I explained this idea in *Fantasy Football for Smart People: How to Cash in on the Future of the Game*:

> *In any set of random (or near-random) data, you'll see lots of "abnormal" results. If you assign Calvin Johnson a 50 percent chance of going for 100 yards and a touchdown in any given game, he'll probably wind up with somewhere around eight games with such numbers over the course of a season.*

> *But there's also a solid chance that he'll appear to have either an unusually outstanding or a very poor year. With a 50 percent chance of 100 yards and a score in any game, Megatron is around as likely to have either five or 12 stellar games as he is to have exactly eight.*

*Because the number of games in an NFL season is so low, it's really easy to see patterns in data that aren't really there. Over the course of even a few NFL seasons, we'd expect some players to appear to have a huge degree of weekly consistency, even if consistency were completely random.*

*Similarly, even with total randomness, a handful of players would appear to be "all-or-nothing" fantasy options without much consistency, when in reality they possess just as much consistency as the most reliable performers.*

I really believe daily fantasy players as a whole place too much stock in past game-to-game consistency on the individual level, especially in the NFL. It's not that game-to-game consistency doesn't exist, but just that it's going to be really, really difficult for us to separate it from randomness.

It's the same reasoning behind my typically bullish stance on injury-prone players. Are some players more likely to get injured than others? Probably, but that doesn't mean we can turn that idea into actionable information.

Injuries are relatively low-frequency events controlled heavily by randomness, and humans aren't built to properly deal with randomness. We perceive all sorts of signals that aren't really there because it's not all that evolutionarily beneficial to say "I don't know."

But in daily fantasy sports, saying "I don't know" is a great thing; by factoring your own fallibility into your decisions—a choice that's reflected in your stance on week-to-week consistency and injury-proneness alike— you'll be able to acquire value where others are overlooking it.

The bottom line is that the majority of what most think they see as consistent play is noise. It would take years of NFL data to establish individual player consistency to the point that we can trust what we're seeing isn't just randomness. By that time, it's too late.

The crux of my individual-player-consistency-is-kind-of-overhyped-but-maybe-not-completely argument is that a small sample size hinders our ability to obtain meaningful results.

The solution? Once again, it's player comps. By broadening the potential player pool to include players who resemble the one in question, we can actually acquire more significant results. Ultimately, it just comes down to figuring out which sorts of players—and which aspects of their games—are consistent and repeatable.

### Quarterbacks

Many NFL teams covet versatility, particularly on the offensive side of the ball, because it can create matchup problems. As a daily fantasy football player, your search for versatility should be more league-specific.

Namely, versatility is a wonderful thing in head-to-head matchups or leagues with a high percentage of players cashing (50/50s and even three-team leagues, too). Versatility increases the number of ways a player can beat a defense, raising his floor.

At the quarterback position, mobile quarterbacks like Cam Newton and Michael Vick have proven to be more consistent than the average passer. That flies in the face of conventional wisdom, which suggests that quarterbacks who rely on their legs are actually big risks.

I looked at the number of quality starts from mobile passers—those who have rushed for over 400 yards in a season—with "quality start" being defined as any game in which the quarterback posted at least six percent of his total fantasy points. That way, I could automatically adjust for differences in total production to see which passers have a flatter distribution of scores, i.e. more consistency.

It turns out that the mobile passers have been just under 10 percent more consistent than pocket passers. The idea that a player like Newton is volatile, which probably stems from the perception that he might not be an elite passer, is just wrong.

### Running Backs

As I mentioned earlier, I was very bearish on Marshawn Lynch heading into the 2013 season. I ended up looking like an idiot, but part of my reasoning was that Lynch was becoming somewhat situation-dependent in Seattle. He had thrived because the Seahawks were a winning team, which is why he saw 338 touches in 2012.

Prior to 2013, though, Lynch hadn't caught more than 28 passes in a season since 2008. It's not like he was a Michael Turner-esque receiver out of the backfield, but Lynch didn't generate a large percentage of his points as a pass-catcher. And with young pass-catching backs behind him on the Seahawks' depth chart, it stood to reason that Lynch might see a dramatic decline in usage if Seattle were to lose more games than expected.

Lynch silenced his 2013 doubters, but that doesn't mean there wasn't a certain level of volatility inherent to his game. As it turns out, pass-catching running backs have proven to be far more consistent than running backs who don't see heavy work as receivers.

Looking at all backs with at least 750 rushing yards, the top 25 percent in catches have been 14.4 percent more consistent than the bottom quarter in receptions. The typical pass-catching running back has generated 10.3 quality starts—defined the same way as with quarterbacks—per season.

Whenever you're analyzing a player, you need to envision how the course of the game could affect his production. In head-to-head leagues in which consistency is king, you want players who can produce almost regardless of the path of the contest. Someone like Reggie Bush can give you numbers even when his team is down 21 points—perhaps to an even greater degree than when they're winning—whereas a back like DeAngelo Williams can be rendered useless.

Further, because running backs who don't catch passes have limited ways to score fantasy points, they're more touchdown-dependent than pass-catching backs. Touchdowns are relatively volatile, so it makes sense to fade backs who lack versatility when you're seeking consistency.

## Wide Receivers and Tight Ends

When I first started studying the week-to-week consistency of pass-catchers, I thought that receivers who are relatively dependent on big plays—think Josh Gordon or Torrey Smith—might be slightly less consistent than receivers and tight ends with shorter targets.

That's true to an extent, but what seems to matter most is the actual alignment. Receivers who play primarily in the slot have recorded over 15 percent more quality starts than those who play out wide.

Why? It's tough to say for sure. Shorter targets (and thus a higher catch rate) probably have something to do with it, but it's also more difficult to double-team a slot receiver (or a tight end). Whereas cornerbacks can use the sideline to their advantage against an X or Z receiver with safety help over the top, nickel cornerbacks need to cover slot receivers all over the field, typically without help.

Ultimately, it seems like slot receivers possess more consistency than outside receivers. That could make them quality options in the flex position for heads-up leagues, especially on full PPR sites like DraftKings.

## NFL Salary Cap Allocation

When I asked DraftKings to look into their database for me, one of the topics about which I had the most excitement was salary cap allocation—how the best teams allocate their salary cap among the various positions.

Well, here's that data for head-to-head games.

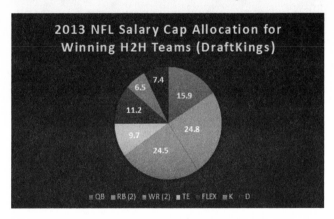

Using DraftKings' $50,000 NFL salary cap, here's how that pie chart breaks down at each position:

**QB:** $7,950

**RB (2):** $12,400 ($6,200 per)

**WR (2):** $12,250 ($6,125 per)

**TE:** $4,850

**FLEX:** $5,600

**K:** $3,250

**D:** $3,700

Now let's compare these numbers to those for the typical winning 50/50 lineup.

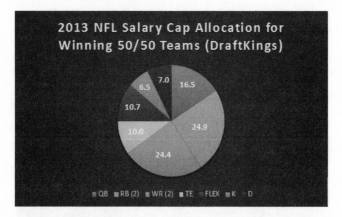

Similar, but we see more money spent at quarterback, less on the flex, and less on the defense. This could just be noise, but don't forget my previous hypothesis that many players are approaching 50/50s in the wrong way. By seeking high-upside lineups, they're increasing the value of a high floor even more.

We know that quarterbacks are consistent options from week to week, so this could be evidence that 50/50s are indeed safer than head-to-head leagues (even after adjusting for the larger sample of lineups) due to the risk-seeking manner in which many players approach 50/50s.

On a side note, it's important to mention that if you're heading into each week picking the players at each position with salaries that most closely match the percentages, you're going to be in trouble. Each week is different, so it would be foolish to bypass a specific value just because it would "mess up" your salary cap allocation.

Instead, I think the chart has value over longer periods of time. At the end of each season, analyze your lineups to see how you distributed available funds. Over larger samples, the intricacies of each individual week should even out, so your allocation should come close to resembling the average winning salary cap distribution.

If you're paying way more for a certain position than normal—say, 20 percent of your cap on quarterbacks—it might be a sign to at least analyze what you're doing to make sure you're seeing the necessary return on your investment at each position.

# 100% EXCLUSIVE OFFER FIRST-TIME DEPOSIT BONUS

**CLAIM MY BONUS »**

**DRAFTKINGS.COM • 1-DAY FANTASY SPORTS**

★ Play free or paid contests and win real money!

★ Daily leagues in all major sports

★ No season-long commitment

★ Over $50 million paid out and counting

★ DraftKings is based in the USA and is 100% legal